THE PROFIT ACCELERATOR
FOR SMALL BUSINESS

DAWN KENNEDY

First paperback edition January 2021

Cover Design by Marie Miller
Cover photo: iStock

ISBN 978-1-7362086-0-1 (paperback)
ISBN 978-1-7362086-1-8 (ebook)

www.entremoneycoach.com

To Mike, thanks so much for this amazing adventure.
We are still arriving, just at a different terminal.

MY GIFT TO YOU

A Gift for You

This book will help you take control of your business finances, get organized, make more sales, and keep more profit in your business. To help you get the most out of your experience there are worksheets throughout the book to guide you. But who wants to write in their book? Am I right?

Download your companion workbook by visiting
   https://entremoneycoach.com/workbook

Questions? Email us at
   assist@entremoneycoach.com

CONTENTS

PROLOGUE

I didn't write this book based solely on training and theory. My husband and I lived and experienced a closed business and financial stress based on our lack of good money management. I wish back in 2013 I was doing everything I do and teach now about business finances. Here is our story.

WHEN MIKE WANTED to start a consulting business in 2011, I was so excited. And it was great. It really was. We followed the state guide, took all the legal steps, got our business license, and set up our office space in our home. Then we took courses through the Small Business Administration and met with awesome advisors through the Service Corps of Retired Executives (SCORE). In short, we followed the "rules."

WE HAD A BUSINESS PLAN, a website, worked hard, read everything, learned a lot, made a ton of rookie mistakes, embraced them, kept going. After about a year or so, we thought we had it figured out. And for the business, we sorta did. But today we talk about UNEQ Consulting (pronounced unique), LLC, in the past tense.

THE PHONE CALL that changed everything in our life and business came at about 5:30pm on November 1st, 2013. I had just returned with food to my motel room in Macon, Georgia, 3 hours from my home, where I was to spend the night before my law student ethics exam at Mercer University the next morning. It was my oldest son on the line telling me, "Mom, Mike fell off a ladder and it's bad."

IN THAT INSTANT, everything changed. Mike's accident was bad. He had four skull fractures, a severed eighth cranial nerve, he lost his hearing in his left ear completely and 60% in the right. It was so bad he spent months in the hospital in a medically induced coma and at the Shepherd Center Rehabilitation Hospital. Mike then started three years of physical, occupational, neuropsychological, and vestibular rehabilitation.

AND OUR BUSINESS, UNEQ Consulting, LLC closed. In an instant. We had to return the rest of the year's (and the 2014) contracts and close it all down. And we were a financial mess. We made over $200k a year, but we were in such financial disarray that I had returned to work at a job in August, so we had at least one steady paycheck. The blessing in that is that we had medical insurance, which would ultimately cover almost $250,000 in surgeries, medical care and rehabilitation related to the accident.

. . .

WHILE OUR BUSINESS looked really good on the profit and loss statement, in reality, we were a cash flow mess. So much so that we accumulated about $50,000 in credit card debt and had an IRS tax lien for $27,000 placed on our house for unpaid self-employment taxes.

HERE'S why our story is important. It's about what we didn't do, and really never thought about. It's our mistakes in not protecting our family and livelihood first as self-employed small business owners. I am sharing so that you can make different decisions.

So, here's a short list of what we wish we had known or done:

- Had a management reserve, or emergency fund with three months of our Breakthrough Number saved in it, so we could take regular paychecks for a while
- Had some sort of disability insurance on Mike, or "business continuity" or Key Man insurance
- Understood that unemployment insurance is for the employed; just not the self-employed
- And that Social Security has an "exclusionary" period of around five months, where even if you are approved for disability benefits, there is no back pay
- Not incurred unnecessary debt. For example, credit cards "we paid off every month." We paid them every month until the income ran out, the deductibles started needing to be paid, and I had to choose. But we weren't doing that. Sometimes our basic expenses went on the plastic and that was a big mistake.

THIS IS why I coach entrepreneurs to avoid the financial mistakes we made. I want your business to serve your customers for many years to come. Long after the scary 5-year statistic.

THIS BOOK IS the culmination of years of practice and training, as an attorney, a financial coach, and a business owner. The tips and strategies have helped hundreds of entrepreneurs take control of their finances, become profitable, and grow their business. I can't wait to see how reading this book, and implementing the lessons learned, changes your life and business.

YOUR FINANCIAL PERSONALITY

"If you don't build your dreams, Someone will hire you to build theirs."
Farrah Grey

*T*his book exists to serve entrepreneurs. Its purpose is to help you grow your business into your vision with simple and smart money strategies that anyone can use. I know every entrepreneur starts with a passion project, because if you don't have a passion, what exactly are you bringing into the world? I'm here to support you in your passion.

PASSION IS the key to getting up early and staying late. It is the secret sauce that makes your eyes sparkle as you serve your audience. As you can see, it is a critical component to successful entrepreneurship.

You need to have passion! It's a necessary element, but not the only one. I love this quote by Dixie Gillaspie: "...without passion you'll run out of energy long before your actions yield the desired result." The action portion of entrepreneurship comes from a different place. It comes from decision. That decision keeps you showing up when things get rough or go south for a bit, and your passion will keep you creating, selling, and serving.

By reading this book, you are deciding to get off the financial struggle bus in your business. The Latin root of the word "decision" actually means "to cut off" and when you make a decision you cut off any other choice. "Decide" isn't an action we are supposed to take too lightly, in that there are other choices available and this should be done after careful consideration.

BEFORE WE DIVE into the money stuff, I want you to make a decision about your business. Decide right now that you are going to take the actions in this book to tackle your finances. There are exercises and worksheets designed to help you with organization, getting your numbers, generating more revenue, finding an accountant, and putting your systems in place. The systems that work for you and that you will use.

MAKE that decision and know that you don't have to put the processes in place by yourself. I'm here to help your passion business make more money and keep more profit! In order to do that, we are going to have to address a few reasons that entrepreneurs struggle with their finances and talk about the emotional toll that money issues can cause.

THE ELEPHANT IN THE ROOM: Talking About Money

. . .

I'M on a mission to change the conversation around business money stuff, and that starts with removing the shame we have about money. I talk to business owners every day and there is a single issue that seems universal. They are filled with shame when there is a money mistake or money misstep. Business owners are okay if a marketing promo doesn't have the expected return, or if there is a product that didn't sell. But the moment you ask about or learn about a money thing, the willingness to learn from a business decision turns into an attitude of self-blame and shame. We tend to marinate in the emotion of shame about money stuff, and it is blocking us as entrepreneurs.

RESEARCH PROFESSOR AND SHAME EXPERT, Brene Brown, talks about how shame works,

"THE LESS YOU talk about it, the more you got it. Shame needs three things to grow exponentially in our lives: secrecy, silence, and judgment."

AND BOY ARE we ever secretive and silent about the money stuff. We don't want to talk about it or admit that perhaps we don't know how to manage some things around money. There is almost a universally accepted attitude that money stuff should never see the light of day, and that it is not okay to talk about.

Before I go further, I want to tell you that I get it. Mike and I had severe money management issues in our first business, and I didn't want to tell anyone or admit I needed help. We just needed to make more money, and we'd be fine. Sound familiar?

Well, you can only "out earn your mistakes" for a short time.

They will catch up to you eventually. I'm no longer quiet about our money mistakes. They are on my website, and I talk about them freely. Because I don't want to have shame anymore about money and how my mistakes affect running my business. In reality, it's a chance to grow and learn and become better. But shame proliferates.

HERE ARE three effects of shame on entrepreneurs that contribute to stress, relationship issues and, ultimately, business failure.

Many Business Owners Have Shame Around Things They Don't Know How to Do.

Entrepreneurs, like people in general, sometimes "should" all over themselves. Like, "I should have" had an emergency fund, or "I shouldn't have" ordered that additional thing. Both of those things may be true, but once these types of things are done, they are done. Feeling shameful about our decisions blocks us from growing and learning.

I want to say for the record right now that business money management is not intuitive. Managing cashflow when people pay you late isn't a skill that you magically gain when you open a business. We don't call and ask for an extension on a bill because, as business owners, we should be successful and able to pay everything on time, right?

It doesn't always work that way. Shame is preventing us from getting the help we need, from putting processes in place, from not taking it personally when money stuff hits us in business. It needs to stop. It is hurting entrepreneurs.

Shame Stops People From Getting the Help They Need

"I should already know what to do, I'm just not doing it," is a refrain I've heard enough to make me scream. People think that, because they may "know" something, that they don't deserve help or support to integrate what they need to do into their systems. And it's the feeling of shame surrounding what we expect from ourselves.

We own a business; we need to do it all perfectly. Bunk. So many business owners are in their passion project, without a passion for the business side or the money stuff. They excel at their core business, but not the "other stuff." This doesn't make them poor business owners, or failures, or whatever other negative description you can give. It means that they know and flourish in their zone of genius.

Those business owners can and should get support for the rest of the business stuff. It's smart and protects their livelihood. But many don't, until they get into trouble because they don't want to admit they don't know. Maybe they can't read a profit and loss report from their accountant, so what, but they think they should.

Maybe they don't really understand the roles of the financial experts; accountants, bookkeepers, and payroll specialists, and their role in protecting the bottom line. But they don't ask about these things because, "I ought to know, I'm in business."

Not so. The help you need is available; you can reach out and get support on things that aren't your passion. And you should.

Shame Makes Business Issues Personal, and Traps Entrepreneurs

I think one of the most devastating things about shame and money is that we turn business cycles and events into our own personal money failures. We don't know how to ride the cycles of business and to even plan for how businesses work. They are dynamic. Many small businesses have irregular or inconsistent income months. Many have cycles of feast and famine in their earnings, particularly in the beginning. But this can happen really at any time.

But one of the first places we look when there are business money things is at ourselves. Maybe we did make a mistake. But we refuse to think that there is a learning curve in business. There may be some shame around some decisions, and those feelings of shame continue to hold us in a cycle of personal feelings of failure. In those feelings, we cannot solve problems creatively, seek help and support, and put systems in place to protect the business and prevent future issues.

Who Are You? Your Money Personality

There are four general business money personalities that affect how you manage your money and how you approach any financial issues. Once you figure out who you best relate to, you can see the steps that can help you have a more successful relationship with your business finances. Who do you see yourself in?

1. Annie: It's all on autopay, ignore and pray

THERE ARE a lot of "Annie auto pays" out there in the business world. They have been told to just put it all on the card, set it and forget it. The problem is, they can have cashflow issues because everyone has electronic access to their bank account. The stress comes with overdraft fees and late fees and over limit fees because she doesn't always have the money in the account when she needs it. In a way, she's afraid to look at her money and believes she isn't very good with it. So, she ignores it and deals with the emotional stress every month thinking, "I'm in business, it's supposed to be this way."

2. Sally: Spendthrift and fearful

SALLY OPERATES from a place of financial fear. Constantly calculating and worrying, she will not invest to grow her business. She is so terrified to make a money mistake, she refuses to make financial decisions that involve risk. In effect, Sally is strangling her business's ability to grow and thrive. She stresses over anything that happens with her money. If a client pays late, she's a mess. Her income obsession can block her ability to see an opportunity that is in the future. She has an almost hostile relationship with money, believing that there isn't going to be enough to meet her needs.

. . .

3. Olivia: Out earning mistakes, no planning

THE OLIVIA PERSONALITY believes that she's got it all figured out but, in reality, she is just managing what's right in front of her, without planning or having the bigger picture. Olivias are treading water financially and making short term decisions without a plan. She's making enough each month to pay her expenses but has no visibility on her financials for the future. She puts any shortfalls on the credit card and may not know that her debt is creeping up. In some respects, she may be growing too quickly, without a financial foundation, and just ends up bootstrapping month to month. That bootstrapping causes stress, but she thinks if she just makes more sales, she will be fine. Olivia doesn't see the financial danger she is getting into. She relates to money only with what needs her attention right now.

4. Jessica: Just trying everything and frustrated

JESSICA IS FOLLOWING all of the guidance. Use this spreadsheet or this program. And she is trying to do everything right. The thing is, Jessicas don't understand profit and loss, but they aren't taking the time to really learn the basics. So, she's losing money and is very frustrated. Jessica works so darn hard, but she never keeps any money after the bills and only pays herself sporadically. She has an accountant but doesn't understand the relationship and role of her financial professionals. She doesn't know her numbers, margins, bottom line, but she's really trying to do everything right. Jessica feels like the money stuff is just too complicated and is allowing the finances to rob her of her joy of being an entrepreneur.

. . .

I KNOW each of these personalities well. At one time or another I have had an Annie, Sally, Olivia, and Jessica relationship with my money. Each of these personalities has positives, and unfortunately, negatives. At times, I've been a hybrid of two of them.

My relationship with money has evolved over the years and is still evolving. There is a balance in my life now, between what I call, "the mechanics" of my money and "the mindset" around my money.

YOUR RELATIONSHIP with money can and should evolve, too. As you begin to define how you best like managing your money every month (this book will teach you that) and your money mindset and comfort with money (which I will touch on, but have abundant resources to share), you will see yourself grow into a space that feels, and operates, for your financial success. The personality you identify with now will not represent where you are after reading this book.

MY BUSINESS FINANCIAL Management Process

BUSINESS MONEY MANAGEMENT doesn't have to be intimidating or complicated. I'm going to give you a four-step foundational framework for your business that covers the four key areas that I believe are the most important to help your business thrive financially. This framework can easily be remembered using the mnemonic "DECK."

Discover your Breakthrough Number,
Establish your financial protection,

Create your money management system, and
Keep more profit.

We are going to walk through these steps, and you will come out the other side with your financial DECK stacked for your success.

DISCOVER YOUR BREAKTHROUGH Number

This first step is critical to knowing your numbers. You cannot begin to plan or project anything without knowing your minimum number that you need to bring into your business. This number consists of your four walls of business: access to buyers, critical operating expenses, inventory and product spend, and payroll and payroll expenses. This is the first number that tells you how to be self-sustaining and includes your own paycheck and taxes.

Establish Your Financial Protection

Once you know how much it really costs to stay in business every month (at the bare minimum), how do you protect it? Creating a cyclical fund for annual expenses and an emergency fund are two ways to protect your operating account and monthly cash flow. We will also check out some cash flow strategies that protect your business every month.

Create Your Money Management System

This is the step that many people overlook or ignore because it may seem intimidating. You don't need fancy software or complicated spreadsheets with calculations to manage your money. You must have a system to track what comes in and goes out (every dime) and a system to plan for future expenses and projects. Because you have your breakthrough number already, you know what your minimum expenses are. You add in any debt payments or project costs here, and make sure that you have a written spending plan.

Keep More Profit

My first rule of business is, "Don't lose money." My second rule is, "Keep your profit." The first one everybody gets. It's the second one that people tend to overlook. Once we start making money in our business, we seem to find a place to spend it! It seems that there is this point, a bottleneck if you will, where everything coming in is going out. Knowing your profit on everything you offer is critical to avoiding this issue. You must make profit on everything. We are going to look at mindset, pricing, expenses, and margins to ensure that your business stays profitable.

Maximizing Your Successful Journey to Financial Wellness

I see success in my clients reaching their financial goals, staying protected at their income milestone, paying themselves and having great job satisfaction. If you can remove the stress and uncertainty that can come up around money, I call it a win. But my most successful clients all have three qualities about them that made them "extra" successful. Adopt these following three tips and watch how fast your relationship with your money evolves!

They Have a Goal and a Purpose for Their Money

My most successful clients have a money goal. Saving to buy a building, leaving the 9 to 5 job, opening a day spa in 3 years are all examples of my client's goals and purposes for a set amount of money. These goals aren't fuzzy. They know how much they need, and they have a timeline to make it. If they don't start that way, they get it when we work together.

If your money goal is "as much as possible" or "as much as I need to cover overhead," you likely don't have the same laser focus to create and make money as my most successful clients do. The truth is, as Zig Ziglar tells us, "if you aim at nothing, you'll hit it every time." You need to define and write down your goals with a plan to reach them. Not that plans can't grow, change, and evolve, but if you don't start with one at all, you aren't going to be able to really measure your progress. Commit to setting goals and having a purpose throughout this process.

They Take Immediate Action to Control Their Money

They opened the holding account, they took the utilities off autopay, they started tracking income every day. Some of my clients have done those tasks the same day we have our session! Keeping their laser focus on the goal, they take quick action and have wins immediately.

. . .

I HAVE SEEN LESS success with entrepreneurs who are slower to make necessary changes. The motivation to get it done quickly goes away, and often only about half of the recommendations make it into the business. They may pay their expenses intentionally, but they don't make the time to create a monthly spending plan (budget). My most successful clients commit to making changes with their money quickly, one step at a time, and they follow through right away. Commit to making the changes right away.

THEY CELEBRATE Every Financial Win and Use Them to Stay Motivated

LET'S FACE IT: saving 5 years for a building can get a little boring. Every $200.00 deposit seems tiny in the face of the price for a building. But my most successful clients celebrate every single win, whether it is a deposit into a building fund, or a payday when they proudly sign both the front and the back of their paychecks.

STAYING motivated can be difficult sometimes, and we all have to deal with the sometime lack of motivation. Celebrating the little things brings joy into the process. If you aren't celebrating and doing a little dance after every sale or payday, I challenge you to start today. Find a small money win and recognize it with gratitude.

LET'S Dive in

. . .

WE JUST NEED to make a final commitment to embrace your new money journey. Whether you are starting as an Annie, Sally, Olivia, or Jessica, you will not stay there in your trip through this book. My aim is to make your money management simple and personalized, and something you will stick to (maybe even enjoy). There is no shame or judgment here (remember the IRS lien on my house?) and I will remind you throughout the book to celebrate as you complete each step in the process. Let's get started.

GETTING ORGANIZED

"The speed of your success is limited only by your dedication
and what you're willing to sacrifice."
Nathan W. Morris

*M*y approach actually starts after you have taken a few preliminary steps to establish your business financial identity and you are organized with your expenses. Many of you will be well past this step already; some of you need to start here. Wherever you are in your journey, take a moment and make sure these steps have been completed for your business.

Separate Your Finances

Your business needs its own financial identity. You need a business bank account, checks, and debit card that you will use to manage your business. Your business expenses should be paid from your business accounts, not personal accounts. In the beginning, if you are supporting your business with personal money, you will make deposits into your business account to cover expenses. The first account you need to open is an operating account. This is where all of your deposits will go and from where you will pay the bills. Make sure you have checks and a debit card on your operating account. You will also write yourself paychecks from this account. If you accept monies from an online payment processor, such as Stripe or PayPal, make sure that all of the money you earn is deposited into this account from all sources.

Opening a Business Account: What You Need by Business Type

You can decide how and where you want to open the account for your business. Some of my clients really like using the internet banks; just ensure that they have business checking. If you are looking for a bank locally, and if you conduct business locally it may be a good idea; look for a smaller regional bank or credit union. I'm not a big fan of the mega banks. Below, I've added some basic information and resources around what you generally need to open a business bank account in the US, Canada, and the UK. All research is current as of this book's release, and the links are to government agencies.

If you are a sole proprietor, you can typically open a business checking account in the United States with your Social Security Number (SSN) or Employer Identification Number (EIN). In the UK you can also open a business account without additional documentation as long as you are a sole trader. In Canada, when you register as a sole proprietor, you will receive a tax number that is required to open a business bank account.

If you have another business entity, such as an LLC or a corporation, the bank will require those business formation documents to open an account in the business's name. This is because you have created a separate "entity" from yourself, so the business acts as its own "person", so to speak. In the US your LLC or corporation will have its own EIN, so make sure you apply for one for your business. Same if you register to be a Limited Company in the UK; that documentation to open your business account because your company is also a separate entity. The same for a Canadian Corporation, which will receive a Federal Business Number (FBN) upon formation.

The Employer Identification Number in the U.S. (EIN)

To open a bank account with some banks, you will need an EIN. I recommend you get one right away even if you don't have employees. The IRS uses this number to track your tax stuff when you operate as a business. I want to note that, if you have several sole proprietor ventures, you will have one number you use for all of your tax stuff for each business. The EIN application process is FREE. Watch for the "services" that charge you to help with this. Go directly to the IRS government website: https://www.irs.gov/businesses/small-businesses-self-employed/apply-for-an-employer-identification-number-ein-online. We will cover some other basics of small business taxes in Chapter 7.

The Federal Business Number in Canada

To open a bank account in Canada, you need a Federal Business Number assigned by Canada Revenue Agency if you operate under any name but your own. According to my research, you can register your sole trader or corporation using a business name in the province or territory where it operates: https://www.canada.ca/en/revenue-agency/services/tax/businesses/small-businesses-self-employed-income/setting-your-business/sole-proprietorship.html

Your Unique Taxpayer Reference in the United Kingdom (UTR)

You don't need to open a business bank account if you are operating as a sole trader in the UK. If you have any other business formation, your Unique Taxpayer Reference Number is assigned to a registered business by Her Majesty's Revenue and Customs Agency. To open a bank account in the business name, you will need details of your company's registration at Companies House, your tax and VAT registration details. Here is the official website for all things UK business: https://www.gov.uk/browse/business/setting-up.

If you haven't already, get your business registered and legal, and open that separate business bank account for your operation. Honestly, I have opened a business bank account in about 45 minutes. Generally, ask for a banker who specializes in opening accounts, and the process can be very smooth. It helps you to create a separate financial identity.

Organize Your Business Expenses

Your next task is to get your expenses identified and organized. Remember, you will be paying these from your business operating account every month! You may not have very many to start with, and that's fine, but you need to have a central location with all of your expense information.

This comes from my own experience of throwing out an electric bill one month by accident. I didn't even realize it hadn't been paid. The next month I got the shock of my life, with disconnect warning on the past due amount. Oops. Since then, I have kept a list of all expenses with contact info, due dates, and login information. I keep both a spreadsheet on the computer and a printed-out Word document just in case my computer dies.

Just choose what works best for you: a spreadsheet, a notebook, a file folder with the receipts, and create the following entry for every expense you pay:

- Name of company & purpose
- Account number
- Date payments are due
- Online login information
- Phone number(s) for the company
- Physical address for mailing a check or other correspondence

I also keep my monthly expenses listed separately from my annual and semi-annual ones, but I note all of them, including any annual subscriptions and when they renew. This list will help you with two things: creating a monthly spending plan, and as a resource for managing your expenses. Additionally, in the future, if you decide to hire a business manager or other support for your business you can just hand off this list (keep it updated) to the person responsible for making sure the bills are paid. They will have the login info and due dates and it will be seamless for your operations. If something comes up, the contact information is readily available, no Google searching required.

Managing the Business and Personal Money Separately

The final step before we dive into my unique Breakthrough Number approach for your business money management is to discuss how to keep the finances separated in practice. Your personal and business finances are different, and you should have a management system for each. The systems do not have to be complicated.

As we walk through my Breakthrough Number method, I will also cover some tips for personal finances, particularly when you rely on the business to pay your personal expenses. For now, as we get started, here are a few basics you should have for your personal money management that will help you set up your business processes.

How Much Personal Income Do You Need?

First, tally up your personal "four walls" because these expenses get paid first, always. The four walls concept comes from Dave Ramsey's personal financial approach https://www.daveramsey.com/get-started . I trained as a financial coach in the Ramsey Method and love this four walls analogy, designed to help you to protect what is inside the box, or house, before you take care of anything outside the box.

Your walls are food, utilities, housing, and transportation. Figure out your number now. This is the minimum amount of money you need to eat, bathe, sleep in a real bed, and get to work so you continue to make money. Know this number.

Next, add together your minimum debt payments. You will have two numbers: the "four walls" number and the "total I need to pay everything" number.

KNOW When Your Bills Are Due

TO ENSURE your finances are solid, know when your personal expenses are due. What is owed by the 1st? the 21st? Make yourself a list. To make things smoother in your personal finances, we are going to schedule your paydays. We are going to say NO to co-mingling! So, you won't pay your car insurance from your business account (unless it's truly a business expense).

Begin to Plan Your Spending

Once you have regular paychecks scheduled, along with the list of bills and when they are due, you can create a personal spending plan (or budget) for what needs to be paid and when. You can plan your personal spending for everything. My only rule for my clients is, write it down. Your plan. It may change, but you will have the baseline as a reference.

Following these steps will allow your business money to function for your business, and your personal finances to work for you personally. We will discuss more strategies later that will help you keep things organized and your two financial lives independent from each other.

Action Steps for Getting Organized

1. Separate your business and personal finances

2. Have a business bank account

3. Create a single list for all of your expenses, including online login information and contact info.

4. Have a separate money management system for the business and personal finances

DISCOVER YOUR BREAKTHROUGH NUMBER

❦

"Money, like emotions, is something you must control to keep
your life
on the right track."
Natasha Munson

*I*t's time to get down to your financial business. When the Breakthrough Number (B-Number) process was developing, I used it for the easy visualization of protecting the inside of your business four walls. It was first created to support a client who knew of the Dave Ramsey "7 Baby Steps" approach to personal finance. Each of the walls I identified for business helped her make decisions on how to spend money and to put processes in place for money management. Over time, I continued to use the approach over and over and finally gave the process a name; The Breakthrough Number, because I realized that everything above this number is a breakthrough to profit to be used for debt, growth, and investing to build the business. This approach is simple, with simple calculations (and not too many of them) and you will know your minimum monthly amount of money the business must bring in, reducing stress and uncertainty.

Why Do I Need My "B" Number?

Because you need to know what you HAVE to make each month, and once you make it, you are into the "gravy." The gravy is the money you decide to park into the categories that meet your obligations and goals. Not to mention the stress you WON'T have worrying about whether you made enough this month! Let's jump in!

Before anything else, you must prioritize your business income to *pay the expenses that keep your business running*. These expenses can be categorized into the four walls. Each of the walls secures one area critical to your business to keep the doors open. These walls are prioritized and paid before anything else is. Added together, these walls create the "B" number.

The Four Walls Consist of:

1. Rent or internet, and utilities, your access to your buyers
2. Critical Operating Expenses that are required to keep doors open
3. Inventory or products to sell or provide services with
4. Payroll and payroll expenses

IF THERE ARE other bills and expenses, such as debt, loans, non-essential subscriptions and things that are part of your financial picture but do not directly impact your ability to make money in business, they are further down the list of expenses.

HERE'S WHY: if you had slower than expected sales for a few months, and you have to choose between the minimum credit card payment and the internet, and you absolutely need the internet to make sales, you will have to prioritize the internet *or you will shut off the direct lifeline between the ability to make money, and not making a dime.*

YOUR UNIQUE BREAKTHROUGH **Number**

LET'S dive in now to discover your unique number. I want to remind you that your business is unique to you. You have a personal stamp on it that no one else has. In that vein, there isn't a "right" number or type of expenses at the stage of business you are in. If you have blanks left, that's fine. And you can, and should, repeat this process when business conditions change, to ensure that nothing gets missed.

When you consistently hit this number every month, you have a breakthrough to profit! Your business has crushed the first hurdle: sustaining itself.

1. **A. The first wall: Rent and utilities or similar expenses**

WHETHER YOU ARE A PRODUCT BASED, service based, or some other venture such as a vehicle-based business, you must FIRST pay the expenses that keep the doors open.

For example, If you are in ecommerce, but didn't pay your internet and domain expenses, you cannot reach the customers who buy from you and they can't find you. If you have a "brick and mortar" boutique, and the landlord locks the door for non-payment, you cannot sell to customers.

NEXT, you must have lights, heat (even in your own home), and in most cases a phone to operate. If you can keep the door open, but don't have electricity, heat, or a way to communicate with your clients, you are not open.

EXPENSE:_____
Amount:_____
    Expense:_____
Amount:_____
    Expense:_____
Amount:_____
    Expense:_____
Amount:_____
    Expense:_____
Amount:_____
    Expense:_____
Amount:_____

TOTAL Up Your First Wall Expenses: _____

1. B. The second wall: Critical operating expenses

THESE ARE the expenses for the services or goods you absolutely require to continue doing business, no matter what! I pay monthly amounts for my cloud-based software, payment system and Zoom account. These are critical to my business operation.

I cannot operate without accessing files and having my clients access them, take payment for services, or the ability to videoconference with my clients. These

expenses, if not paid, would shut me down very, very quickly. These expenses go, "next," making up wall two.

These are the "critical" expenses, meaning that I cannot operate without them.

THINK:
- Payment services
- Insurance
- Software on a monthly subscription
- Gas for your car if you travel

ANOTHER NOTE ON "CRITICAL BUSINESS EXPENSES." Many of us start out with certain expenses that are important to us, maybe logo items for example, that we think are "critical", but they really aren't. If the expense isn't absolutely critical to providing your clients with legendary service, it is not part of your second wall. Your second wall should be as "lean" as possible.

. . .

I WANT you to think of your business money in terms of longevity. Think staying power. I got rid of a software program called, "PDF Filler" because, even though it was a fantastic program, I just didn't use it that much, so it ended up being "nice to have." *If you don't use something each and every month, it may be more cost effective to cancel a subscription, and just pay for a single use, if and when you need it.*

AND, at the risk of offending some people here, this means managing your money over the long term, perhaps when the novelty of what you do, make, sell, wears off. Time to be objective! Can I operate without this? If not, it goes on this list.

EXPENSE:_____
Amount:_____
    Expense:_____
Amount:_____
    Expense:_____
Amount:_____
    Expense:_____
Amount:_____
    Expense:_____
Amount:_____
    Expense:_____
Amount:_____
    Expense:_____
Amount:_____
    Expense:_____
Amount:_____

. . .

TOTAL YOUR SECOND WALL EXPENSES: _____

1. C. The third wall: Inventory and products you need

SEEMS ALMOST OBVIOUS, but if you don't have anything to sell, you can't make money. If you are in a business that sells or creates products, you probably need either to get inventory to sell, or raw materials to create what you sell. For example, if you resell on eBay, you must have things to sell. If you make tee shirts, you probably need, at a minimum, the blank shirts and vinyl. In a service business, such as a lash or hair salon, you need products that are required to complete your services. The key here, when money is tight (and it may be, some months), is to *be reasonable in purchasing inventory.*

BUY ONLY what you need to sell, plus a little for new customers or clients. One mistake many business owners make is having overestimated their needs. Having stock or product lying around that isn't being sold is *money sitting on a shelf* that could have been used for other things.

THINK about your *highest volume sellers, highest profit margin items, and long lead time items* you want to keep on hand.

IF YOU DO brisk business and need to reorder, identify your long lead time items, the ones that take the longest to receive, and perhaps keep more of those, but less of the items you can have shipped within a few days. These products and numbers will change, no worries, just keep an idea of how much you use and reorder each month, so you can plan to keep money on hand to replenish if you have an odd income cycle.

SPECIAL NOTE: If you are a boutique or other business that changes inventory on a regular basis: you may have to order and plan seasonally, so this can be tricky. Many boutique owners have relationships with other owners to buy and sell excess inventory, or with vendors who can take reorders as needed.

- Purchase what you NEED, and don't overdo it when money is tight
- You may have to purchase a few months out for the season, and payment won't be due until inventory ships
- The money due when the apparel ships will be put into an account (and not touched) as if you paid it today. That is your cost to set aside in this category

SPECIAL NOTE FOR E-COMMERCE SELLERS: you have the additional expense of shipping

- Any shipping costs need to be figured into this category, because customers won't purchase if they don't receive their merchandise!
- Put this as a line item into your spending plan. I know, I know, clients pay shipping
- But you need to purchase packing supplies and boxes up front to have on hand, and if you use logo anything

for shipping, you cannot risk running out. Do not
short yourself here

ITEM/   product: _____
cost:_____
   Total   sold   last   month:_____
Notes:_____

ITEM/   product: _____
cost:_____
   Total   sold   last   month:_____
Notes:_____

ITEM/   product: _____
cost:_____
   Total   sold   last   month:_____
Notes:_____

ITEM/   product: _____
cost:_____
   Total   sold   last   month:_____
Notes:_____

ITEM/   product: _____
cost:_____
   Total   sold   last   month:_____
Notes:_____

1. **Notes:**

D. THE FOURTH WALL: Payroll and payroll taxes

IF YOU DO NOT HAVE employees yet, but you pay yourself, you want to complete this estimate! By the way, **you get paid before debt.** Trust me, you do. *You* are a business expense.

IF YOU HAVE EMPLOYEES, *they get paid before you.* Period. We've all heard stories of paychecks bouncing. Never let that be you. If you have employees, but things get VERY tight, and you must lay off, even temporarily, *your employees will appreciate that you paid them always, and on time.* Pay your payroll taxes as well.

THIS IS an important wall of your business to figure even if you don't have employees yet. Use this section as a planning tool when you are looking to add employees, as this should be a guide for what you can really afford to pay your team. You need to know what this expense will be (generally) so you can plan and put enough in the management reserve.

TO FIGURE out your fourth wall, you need to determine:

1. Hourly wages or salary by position, including yours
2. Gross weekly or bi-weekly wages
3. Your portion of employer taxes
4. Your personal tax withholding for self-employment

IF YOU ARE the only employee for your business, set aside the proper amount of self-employment taxes for the pay period. *You must write yourself a business check for your reasonable salary, don't just take from the till.* You won't want to **take all** of your net profit for personal bills. You will want to hold some back to cover your "B" Number in wonky sales months.

WORKSHEET 1: How Much are You Paying?

HOW OFTEN WILL or do you pay employees (including yourself)? _____ (every week, every 2 weeks, etc...)- You will need this for Monthly Estimates.

HOW MUCH WILL or do you pay per hour/or a salary? _____

IF YOU HAVE different hourly pay amounts for different roles, describe them and give amounts here:

SELF:_____
    Employee: Description: _____ cost/hr
_____

    Employee: Description: _____ cost/hr
_____

    Employee: Description: _____ cost/hr
_____

Employee: Description: _____
cost/hr_____
    Employee: Description: _____   cost/hr
_____

WORKSHEET 2: Estimates for each payday

YOU NEED to multiply the hourly wage by the number of hours, to estimate the gross wages **you will pay per payday**. EX: if you pay weekly, and you have an employee making $12.00/ hr. for 10 hours, the gross per week is $122.00 for each individual.

SELF:_____
    Employee: per hour:_____ estimated hrs: _____-
cost _____
    Employee: per hour:_____ estimated hrs: _____-
cost _____
    Employee: per hour:_____ estimated hrs: _____-
cost _____
    Employee: per hour:_____ estimated hrs: _____-
cost _____
    Employee: per hour:_____ estimated hrs: _____-
cost _____
    Estimated gross pay total for payroll **every pay period**:
_____

IF THERE IS an odd income fluctuation, looking at your gross pay for each employee per pay period may be a good way to make scheduling adjustments, if needed.

. . .

WORKSHEET 3: Other Payroll Costs for You as an Owner or Employer:

AS AN EMPLOYER, you will have additional out of pocket costs above the hourly wage. This often comes as a surprise to new employers because we understand tax withholding from the employee is when we deposit their federal and state taxes. If you are a US employer, withhold your portion of Social Security and Medicare. Your withholding for your employees is in addition to their hourly pay. So, if you pay $10.00/hour you must also pay a percentage of that cost out of pocket for your portion of withholding.

IN THE US you must pay a percentage of the employees' Social Security and Medicare, and that is around 15.56% of the gross pay. They pay 7.78%, you pay 7.78% to equal the withholding required. For yourself, you will need to withhold the entire amount from your checks.

WHAT IS YOUR WITHHOLDING NOW, or likely to be?
Amount of withholding **per pay period**:

SELF:_____
Employee: gross: _____ + withholding: _____ = cost
_____
Employee: gross: _____ + withholding:_____ = cost
_____
Employee: gross: _____ + withholding:_____ = cost
_____

Employee: gross: _____ + withholding: _____= cost
_____

Employee: gross: _____ + withholding: _____ = cost
_____

Employee: gross: _____ + withholding: _____ = cost
_____

ADD the total withholding for each person. This way, you can get an estimate of your total payroll costs per pay period
_____

WORKSHEET 4: Monthly Estimates

TAKE the Worksheet 3 total_____ and multiply by the number of pay periods in a month.

**IF you pay every two weeks, multiply by 2, or every week, multiply 4, to determine *your estimated gross monthly payroll* costs: _____

THIS IS the monthly amount that you should anticipate for your payroll and withholding, unless you either reduce or increase hours for your employees.

TOTAL FOR WALL 4:_____

NOTES:

. . .

ADD TOGETHER the Business Four Walls

LIST THE TOTALS for each wall:
Wall 1: _____
Wall 2: _____
Wall 3: _____
Wall 4: _____
Total Breakthrough Number: _____
Congratulations! You now have your B-Number!

THIS IS the minimum amount your business must make for one month. This number is what you need to be fully self-sustaining, including your own check! Once you have this amount each month, all other income is yours to decide how to use.

ADDITIONAL BENEFITS of Having Your Breakthrough Number

HERE ARE a few more additional benefits to expect when you take the time to do the (easy) calculation of your Breakthrough Number.

MORE ACCURATE WHOLESALE COSTS

I'VE WORKED with several business owners who forgot something...some small or easily forgotten expense that affected their profit margin. Running through each of the walls carefully uncovered things like the cost of blank labels and ink for handmade products. That cost was easily overlooked because it was under $25.00/month, but it needs to be included because it affects the real cost to the business and needs to be recovered.

FINDING HIDDEN MONEY AND A CHANCE TO BECOME LEANER

THE FIRST TIME this happened I was actually in an airport helping a friend run through the breakthrough number process. We were discussing her critical operating expenses and remembered that she had a service she paid for every month that she was no longer using! This service was about $100.00/ year. More than once I have seen clients eliminate or change services and expenses when they take a hard look at deciding what is critical and what is just "useful."

MORE CONFIDENCE IN MAKING STRATEGIC BUSINESS DECISIONS

THIS BENEFIT WAS SORT OF foreseeable in that I knew people could use the process to calculate different scenarios such as hiring new people or adding a service because they would be able to forecast the new expense's impact on the money. But the way my client uses it to make decisions is quite surprising! She literally just uses her known monthly B-number amount to help her make decisions. Her breakthrough number is about $5k a month and includes her personal paycheck. Anytime she wants to do anything different, she looks at how much *she made over her number that month* and how much she has in the bank. She can then say, "Oh, this is okay, I made an extra $2k and I can still pay myself for 3 months." That was her quick "back of the envelope" calculation for hiring her part-time virtual assistant and a business coach. Amazing!

YOUR ALL-IN NUMBER

NOW I BET you are wondering when we are going to talk about the other expenses and any business debt. I didn't forget. The Breakthrough Number covers all of the priorities for your business to keep it open and operating every month. The All-In Number contains everything else, plus the B-Number so your business is All-In. Let's grab that figure right now.

LIST all of your other MONTHLY business expenses. We will address irregular expenses and annual costs in Chapter 5 (the C-fund). Include any debt expenses and minimum payments. We will also address debt reduction strategies in Chapter 5.

EXPENSE:_____
Amount:_____
    Expense:_____
Amount:_____
    Expense:_____
Amount:_____
    Expense:_____
Amount:_____
    Expense:_____
Amount:_____
    Expense:_____
Amount:_____

Expense:_____

Amount:_____

Expense:_____

Amount:_____

Total Additional Monthly Expenses and Debt:_____

ADD TO THE BREAKTHROUGH NUMBER. Your All-In
Number:_____

THESE ARE the two numbers you need right now to get started
managing your business finances. You will use these numbers as
the base of your emergency fund and debt snowball (Chapter 5),
for pricing and profit decisions (Chapter 6), and for decisions
on business loans and investments (Chapter 9). Even if you were
to stop right here, you still have a good basis upon which to
make future financial decisions. Just run the Breakthrough
Number Process whenever you are considering a financial
change that will add to or subtract monthly expenses from your
business.

ACTION STEPS:

1. Calculate Your Breakthrough Number

2. Evaluate any expenses that you may not need and elimi-
nate them

3. Post your number where you will see it, this is your
first goal

4. Calculate Your All-In Number

MONEY MECHANICS TO PROTECT YOUR CASH

"Never take your eyes off the cash flow because it's the life
blood of business."
Richard Branson

*I*n the last chapter, we discovered the minimum amounts of money you need to bring in every month to be a self-supporting business. Here, we are putting in the mechanics of actually managing every bit of money that comes in, so you are in control and empowered with your money management. It is extremely important that you get into the habit of controlling and protecting your cash. Creating your money management system is the "C" in my four DECK Pillars.

THE KEY IS to find the style that works best for you and that you will stick to. In my approach you are not required to use spreadsheets or software unless you like them and are comfortable using them. I have a few very successful clients who write their income and expenses on a monthly calendar or a paper template and it works for them. Because they are consistent with it. They would NOT be successful with another method, and that is perfectly fine. Here, you need "to do you" in order to make a permanent and sustainable change.

Be Intentional With Your Money

If you aren't already, this is the time to manage cash flow very carefully. You need to be in control of your cash. The first step for mastering your cash is to become very intentional with your money. This means to take as much as you can off of auto-pay. I know this flies in the face of the "set it and forget it" philosophy, but I want you controlling every single dime that you can. I also know that some monthly subscriptions, like Zoom, require a monthly recurring charge to the card. But your utilities don't, and get those debt payments off of there as well.

Do not give anyone electronic access to your checking account if you can help it. I am very familiar with the heart sinking feeling that comes with realizing someone took a payment and you are now in the red in the operating account. Using over-draft protection isn't a good monthly business strategy. The next time you make a deposit, the bank takes it's overdraft fee first, leaving your deposit smaller than expected. Ugh.

Another strategy that you can use when you revoke everyone else's access is that you can hold bills for a few days or partial pay some expenses, without penalties, if money gets tight. Holding the water bill for a day or two while you are waiting for an invoice to be paid keeps cash in your pocket, just in case. I have paid a utility bill in two payments before, and it kept much needed cash in the business a little bit longer. Resist the urge to run your business out of cash each month. You will have late paying clients, you will get chargebacks, you will have months when there is a bank holiday, and your deposit is delayed. Expect it. And commit to staying in control.

INCOME PROJECTIONS, Cash and Sales

MONEY HAS to come into the business in order for you to pay your expenses from your business account. I want to briefly talk about how you need to look at your business income and how to create an income projection for your monthly spending plan. If you were to receive a check from an employer every two weeks, it would be pretty simple to plan because you know how much money you had coming in. It really isn't that simple in the beginning, but we can make it very straightforward.

LET'S take a minute and talk about the difference between "sales" and "cash." When you make "sales" in your business and the customer pays in full, the sales amount equals the cash in. But if you put the client on a payment plan, the sales amount is the total value sold, but the cash in is ONLY THE MONTHLY PAYMENT. This is important to note because we see sales announced online as,"5k, 10k, 20k a month" but that may not actually be the cash collected by the business in the month of the sale. I want you projecting CASH IN: the cash you will have available for expenses, growth, and protection.

· · ·

IF YOU HAVE EXPECTED RECURRING income every month, such as memberships, start with that number as your income. If you have payments due on payment plans, know what's due and add that. I recommend that you have a percentage of your customers and clients on a recurring payment basis or on a payment plan. You can get clients on a monthly payment plan for seasonal services, as well. I want you to have predictable, reliable income streams in your business. Do not shy away from having monthly income that you can count on.

IF YOU DO NOT HAVE any revenue that is on a recurring monthly basis or any payment plans that will be paid, you will need to estimate the income from your upcoming sales. You can do that by looking at your historical sales and also by the percentage of time you convert a new customer or client from nurturing a sale.

IN THE VERY beginning it may seem like a struggle to try and figure out how much you should bring in. I get it. I have been there. The best thing you can do is keep collecting data and getting better about reaching your audience and getting people to buy your product or service. This is not a book about sales strategies, and I am no expert. If you need help getting sales, find specialized help.

SELECT AND MARK Your Pay Days and Bill Days

Protecting cash means letting it accumulate and leaving it alone, until you need to use it. This means not going into the account every day or two to pay a bill. And as we said, "no" to co-mingling, it definitely means not swiping the business debit card for personal bills. I recommend that you find a few days a month for paying bills and for paydays. For paydays, I like an "every two week" cycle. I have a newsletter that comes out every other Thursday to help entrepreneurs remember to pay themselves and to celebrate two more weeks in business. To sign up, visit https://entremoneycoach.com/payday.

FOR EXPENSES, just pick two days that you will sit down and pay the bills. You can make it the same as your paydays. You can pick two dates (like the 7th and the 20th) or weeks, like the first and third Wednesday. You need to do what works for you. Make sure you look at the bill due dates. Also look at the dates you have recurring income or payment plan payments made. This will help you to know how much you can expect, and when, and plan your paying days around that.

TRY NOT to move your days around once you set them. Try it for at least a quarter to see how it works for your cash, expenses, and tracking strategy. If you do need to make changes based on new lines of recurring revenue, or having a change in expense due dates, try to keep those dates for a while. It takes about 3 months of working on your money strategies to create a habit. Changing every month (or every week) will make it more difficult for you to make a permanent systematic change to your business.

TRACKING **Strategies**

THE NEXT PART of your system is to figure out how tracking works best for you. Once again, you have many different choices of tracking methods. I recommend reconciling your income weekly; in other words, have a day of the week that is the end of your income cycle and write the total that came in over that 7-day period. I have several clients who pick Sunday to do this when they do their weekly business planning.

ONE REASON TO track income weekly is to look at your business cycles and trends. Do you make more in the first week of the month than the third? Have you found that more recurring income products were sold around the 15th instead of the 25th? This data can be very helpful for launching new products and services, as well as planning your sales and marketing.

TRACKING your expenses becomes easier when you set your bill pay and paydays, because those are the days you track what was paid, and how much was spent. There are apps on the phone such as "YNAB" (You Need a Budget), and even though it is designed for personal finances, one of my clients uses it for tracking business income and bills. Maybe you like a spreadsheet? Create one that tracks your expenses, when they are due and when they are paid.

THIS IS where you get to personalize the tracking strategy that works for you, your personality, and your business style. Don't try to rely on memory to tell you where that $65.00 cash payment went. It doesn't have to be a complicated system. You can use a sheet of paper. JUST WRITE IT ALL DOWN. And feel free to get creative! Maybe you use a voice note on your phone at the time you pay bills or make a purchase. Then you write down your purchases on a calendar, template, spreadsheet, or software program once a week. I have a 90-day undated Money Management Planner available, with calendar and templates, that can be used every quarter over and over again.

ONE OTHER NOTE ON TRACKING. Create categories for your "extra money." "Miscellaneous" is the category of money that runs off and spends itself, and we don't want this. I am a firm believer in "profit parking lots" that have names, and a purpose attached. If you buy ink for the computer, note it as "ink" or "office supplies" not "petty cash" or "misc.!"

YOUR MONTHLY SPENDING Plan

NOW WE NEED to plan what gets spent, and when, and put that plan in writing. I don't like the word "budget." I think it seems restrictive, and many people agree. Prefer to use, "the spending plan," because you are truly free to decide how to spend. I find, however, that the monthly spending plan causes some real stress for people. Sometimes it is the idea of planning out the money (particularly before it's made) and sometimes it's the feeling that your plan must be perfectly executed to be any good. BUNK! Having an *idea* of what you will spend, and when, makes it easier to make decisions. Because you have set a limit. A written limit. Your spending plans. And the plan is designed to be dynamic. As dynamic as your business.

Having an idea of what you want to spend every month in different areas of your business is smart. It's way too easy to just hand over the debit or credit card without counting how the amount you spend will reflect on your overall business income and expenses. You are in business to make money and earn a profit. You need to have a plan for your spending.

. . .

Know What You Want to Spend and Write it Down

THINK of your spending plan as a helpful guide. Beyond the expenses in your breakthrough number (the four walls), you should consider your spending in other areas, such as your marketing, projects, support people (not employees), and business processes. Creating a marketing budget, a budget for contractors, and a budget for things like accountants and payroll allows you to make decisions throughout the month on where to maybe spend more, or where to cut back.

How much you can afford to spend will be something you need to work out based on your business's goals and income, but have the numbers written down. I've seen too many businesses hire people or launch a campaign and then run out of money before plans could be completed. Because they bought into what sounded awesome, not what was really affordable at that moment in their business.

Plan to Make Changes Throughout the Month

Guess what? My spending plans RARELY go unchanged throughout the month. Typically, at least one thing changes. Maybe I made a small investment into a resource or course that became available. Or I decided to move a project forward sooner than planned because of an opportunity that I wasn't expecting. The thing is, having a written plan allows me to make those decisions.

Unexpected changes are, well, to be expected. When you have your plan in front of you, you have a baseline. Then consider what comes up. You can ask yourself, "Can I afford this? Is it moving us towards the vision? Does this work better now or later?" Your answers will then guide whether you want to spend now or not. But with a good written plan, you will already know what money has been allocated, what's left, and how much extra has come in the door to guide you.

PLANNING Plans by Personality Type

HERE ARE a few tips for planning while staying aligned with the strengths of your financial personality.

- If you resonate with Annie: Start to get intentional with your money by writing down three things you want to accomplish this month with your finances. Anything counts! Paying your bills on time, paying yourself, taking things off autopay, hiring a new team member, all of it. Put your list where you will see it and check off those things as they happen.

- If you resonate with Sally: Once you create your plan

this month, stick with it! For the whole month. Resist the urge to rethink it and second guess yourself. You have the plan, and you just need to execute it. Trust yourself and your ability to make it happen!

- If you resonate with Olivia: Pick the days you will sit down and reconcile the money. Each week, make sure you are counting *all* the income and *all* the expenses. You will feel so much more in control when you see it in black and white.

- If you resonate with Jessica: Plan your income, not just the spending! Outline your offers and check your profits for each, then backwards plan how many you are going to sell this month. You will be more empowered by having a concrete number of things to sell to make your plan a success.

PROTECTING YOUR BUSINESS

"Strive not to be a success, but rather to be of value."
Albert Einstein

*T*he next pillar of my approach is to Establish Your Financial Protection. These next steps create a financial cushion that protects your business from the ups and downs of income and those unexpected hits. Think COVID-19 in 2020. Think about a fall off a ladder and the business unexpectedly having to close. The fact is, if Mike and I would have had this protective system in place back when we owned UNEQ, we would have been in a much better place. I would have had three months of paychecks coming into our house as we wound down the business.

As we examine each of these strategies, think about implementing them right now, especially if you are early in your business. If you begin to create a habit around anchoring your business with a protective strategy it will be easier to stick with, to fund, and to use when necessary to keep yourself in business.

PROTECT YOUR MONTHLY SPENDING PLAN: **The Cyclical Fund (C-Fund)**

THE CYCLICAL FUND (or C-fund) is a type of sinking account that protects your monthly spending plan by having all of the money you need for annual and semi-annual expenses in the bank when you need it. When you create a C-fund, you will deposit a smaller amount each month towards these costs and save enough over 12 months to have *all of them covered* when they come due! The alternative is what most of us do now, having to pay the large bill all at once *out of one month's income*. That can be quite stressful and hard on your monthly spending plan!

WHEN YOU STOP and really think about it, there are probably a few things that are renewed annually. Do you renew your business license annually? Business insurance? Domain name and SSL certificate? Chances are, you will have an average of five or six important business expenses that keep the doors open.

IT IS important to figure out the non-monthly, but regular expenses that are important for the business. You also need to estimate the amount you will owe, and the month the expense comes due. Then placing the estimated amount of money into a "holding" type account or reserving it separately in your checking account will allow you to have the funds available when the payments are due.

. . .

HERE ARE a few things to consider when starting a C-fund. You can save a little each month for your expected annual expenses:

1. Make sure that, IF you open a separate CHECKING account at the bank, you have a FREE account. Otherwise, service fees will eat up what you put aside and cause you to go a bit backwards. I recommend a small(ish) regional bank or credit union for these accounts.

2. Do NOT open a SAVINGS type account if you will make frequent withdrawals to pay these bills as they come due. In the U.S., "Regulation D" limits the amount of free transfers or withdrawals to six each month. Then the bank can charge a fee for every subsequent withdrawal.

3. In the beginning, you may have a bit of overlap with what's due and what is saved. So, you may have to pay a bit more and continue saving. I know, if you are living paycheck to paycheck, this doesn't always allow much room, but if you don't start soon enough before the next expense, you may have to stretch.

EXAMPLE: You have $85.00 due in three months. You typically put away $21.00/month. In three months, you have $63.00 saved, but are $21.00 short. Pay the $85.00, but still try to put away the $21.00 so you are on track for the next expense due.

. . .

IT's so easy to get frustrated when we forget when the annual bills come due and, of course, they still come due. Consider the Cyclical Fund as a way to put a little away each month to cover what you will need. The stress is really reduced when the amount you need for an expected expense isn't squeezed 100% from the same monthly budget.

YOUR TURN, How Much is Your Monthly C-Fund Deposit?

FOLLOW a simple three-step approach to implement your C-Fund and control your cyclical costs!

1. Complete the worksheet
  • Identify each cyclical expense
  • Estimate the amount you will owe for that expense
  • Note the month due and the frequency you pay it
  • Calculate the amount you must save each month for *each expense*
  • Calculate the total amount of your monthly deposit to *cover all C-costs*

YOU CALCULATE both your costs for each item individually and all costs together because they change! You will only have to adjust one if it goes up or down in cost!

2. Open your holding account. Make sure you open a free or low-cost checking account separate from your operating account for your monthly deposits.

. . .

3. Calendar your Cyclical expenses. The last step is to *enter each of your cyclical expenses on your annual calendar* in the months it is due. Just write them on there so you have a visual reminder of when they get paid. If you use an online calendar, you can set recurring reminders, too!

WORKSHEET for Your Regular C- Fund Deposit

STEP 1. List the Cyclical Expense, the month due, amount you will pay, and how often.

Step 2. Divide the amount by the frequency to determine the *monthly deposit.*

Expense:_____

Month_____ Amount:_____

Every _____ months. Monthly deposit for budget:_____

Expense:_____

Month_____ Amount:_____

Every _____ months. Monthly deposit for budget:_____

Expense:_____

Month_____ Amount:_____

Every _____ months. Monthly deposit for budget:_____

Expense:_____

Month_____ Amount:_____

Every _____ months. Monthly deposit for budget:_____

Expense:_____

Month_____ Amount:_____

Every _____ months. Monthly deposit for budget:_____

Expense:_____
Month_____ Amount:_____
Every _____ months. Monthly deposit for budget:_____

STEP 3. Add together all of your total C-cost here. Total: _____. This is the total you will need in your fund to cover all C-costs in a year.

STEP 4. Divide the total C-cost by 12: _____
This is your total amount to deposit monthly: _____

USE this Quick Checklist for Starting and Maintaining Your C-Fund

- Do I have a holding account (free checking) separate from my operating account to hold my deposits?
- Did I calculate my monthly deposit amount?
- Did I add "C-Fund" as a category to my written monthly spending plan?
- Did I calendar all C-costs in the month they are due?
- Do I know when there will be an overlap between what I saved and what I owe? Have I noted how much that month will cost?
- Do I have a process to add expenses and recalculate the deposit at least once a year?

PROTECTING YOUR BREAKTHROUGH NUMBER: **The Emergency Fund**

THE SECOND LAYER of protection for your business protects your entire operation by creating a cash cushion. Three months of your breakthrough, or B-Number, is a wise amount to put aside in case of emergency. This fund is a stash of cash that covers the entire breakthrough number, including your paycheck. The importance of having extra cash for emergencies cannot be overstated. I have worked with entrepreneurs who spend everything they make each month in profit. They enlarge marketing budgets and add services to their businesses but have no cash to protect their existing milestone.

THE REASON I believe three months is a minimum number is that, if disaster happens, you still have a full quarter to right the ship. You will have expenses and a paycheck for the three months it takes to pivot, to launch, to take corrective action in your business.

AT FIRST THAT number may seem a bit high and, honestly you may be thinking, "I'm barely surviving right now. You want me to save HOW MUCH?" But it is possible to save towards your goal and hit it in a few simple steps.

1. *Get Set Up for Success.* Make sure you have a separate bank account so your emergency fund money doesn't get comingled and accidentally spent. Keep it liquid but keep it separate, even in a different bank. Have a fee free checking account, with checks, for access and

have a defined list of what constitutes an emergency. Some of my clients use money market accounts with checks available for that account.

1. *Put a little in each month.* Make your emergency fund a line item in your budget. If you write down your savings goal, and you write in a goal for saving a certain amount, you are more likely to do it. Save a little each month, and you will be amazed how fast it grows.

1. *Make larger deposits as you make more money.* Alternatively, or additionally, save a portion of your profits over your B-Number in a good month. Let's say that you have a very successful month in sales: commit to stashing some portion of that profit in the fund.

1. Celebrate your progress. You are actively taking steps to protect your business should you need a little money to cover you.

TREAT your emergency fund as a priority and it will be funded faster than you expect. *And once it is funded, you are done!* You won't need to add any more money, and you will have a few months of protection against anything that affects your business. You will then be in a better position to grow and take on new growth and risks, and you'll be more confident knowing you can cover what you need to every month.

TIPS FOR FUNDING Your Emergency Fund by Financial Personality

HERE ARE the best tips to help you fund your emergency fund based on your financial personality! For a brief description of personality types, see Chapter 1.

- If you resonate with Annie: Make your emergency fund savings a line item each month, and be intentional with setting that money aside. You can determine how quickly or slowly you want to fill your fund, divide your goal by the number of months, and get a figure you are comfortable putting away.

- If you resonate with Sally: You are likely looking to get fully funded ASAP! One way to do this is to set aside a specific amount each month, and to designate a percentage of profits (say 10%) as an additional deposit. As an aside, don't let the need to fund this emergency fund be a source of stress. Just commit to making your regular deposits and you will meet your goal sooner than you think.

- If you resonate with Olivia: If you make a deposit every time you pay your other bills, it won't be forgotten, and you will get it done! Just divide your monthly deposit goal in half, and make the emergency fund a line item for every bill pay day.

- If you resonate with Jessica: Commit to depositing a percentage of profits into the account. This will allow you the flexibility to make a monthly deposit after you've completed your reconciliation. I recommend 20-30% of your profits since you aren't depositing a set monthly amount.

IT'S important to note that this emergency fund can also act as a warning for your business, a canary in a coal mine if you will. If you find that you are using this reserve account regularly for overhead expenses (and not just in a slightly down month), it is a good indication that you need to re-examine your business model, pricing, processes, etc., to figure out why you are not generating enough income each month to cover those critical operating expenses.

PROTECT the Health of Your Business: Limit the Debt on Your Business

A WORD of caution on using debt to start or run your business. I run an almost debt free operation, now. I didn't before when my husband and I ran UNEQ Consulting, LLC.

When we lost Mike's income and our business, we stared at the stack of bills we could no longer pay. We were normal! Two car payments, personal and business credit cards, many we kept only for the "points"... we could have paid cash.

BUT THOSE CREDIT cards "we paid off every month" stopped being paid when the medical deductibles started needing to be paid, and I had to choose. We paid everything we owed in full, including the IRS lien on the house (for back self-employment taxes), and have sworn off personal debt. I now proudly run my financial coaching business with very little debt; my only loan was secured by my car. My little bit of debt was for the growth of my business, I didn't take out a loan to start it.

I've had to adjust my own thinking around business versus personal debt over the last year or so. I do believe that businesses need capital at certain points to grow. I was dead set against debt after our past experience with collectors, but, back then, we didn't take debt with a plan and all of it was for Breakthrough Number expenses. In Chapter 9, we will talk about taking out loans to grow your business.

THOUGHTS ON GETTING RID of Debt

IF YOU CURRENTLY HAVE BUSINESS DEBT, THERE is no judgment here. As you read in my own story, I know the position you are in because I was there a short time ago. A word of caution here: to preserve cash in your business, I do not recommend attacking the debt right away and draining your business of its lifeblood cash. I worked with a client who had an amazing month and made almost $30,000. She used that chunk of money to pay off some loans she took to start the business. Two months later, she had a slower sales month, and could barely make her rent on the boutique.

YOU NEED a plan to get out of debt, and it starts by not taking any more on. Prioritize your four walls, so you can keep operating. Fund your sinking fund. Then tackle the debt. I promise that your creditors do not care if you have hot water; they just want their money. So PLEASE make sure you are protecting your operations before you start throwing extra money on debt.

THEREFORE, the business debt snowball becomes a priority ONLY after you are consistently meeting your B-number every month and have at least a month or two of expenses in an emergency fund. The debt snowball helps you clear debt much more quickly than just making minimum payments on it all. A benefit of clearing debt quickly is that you will shrink the liabilities and monthly payments and open up some cash that can be available in case of an emergency.

THE BUSINESS DEBT Snowball

THE DEBT SNOWBALL method is great for tackling debt because you will generate momentum and see results quickly. I learned this method, and used it myself on our debt free journey, and it allowed us to clear $77,000 in 39 months. This process is taught by Dave Ramsey and I find his method of planning your snowball (and getting it done) to be the easiest and best. You will make a commitment to a specific amount each month that will be allocated for debt until it is all paid in full.

. . .

HERE ARE THE BASIC STEPS:

- Step 1: List your debts from smallest to largest amounts. Don't worry about interest rates or payments.
- Step 2: Continue to make all of your minimum payments on all your debts except the smallest one.
- Step 3: Throw as much money as you can on the smallest debt, until it is paid off.
- Step 4: Move to attacking the next debt, adding the payment from the paid off debt to increase your monthly payment amount.

YOU WILL CONTINUE these steps until all the debt is paid. As you go on, the monthly payments get bigger and bigger as each debt payment is rolled into the next one, creating the "snowball." You should sit down and list the bills in order, the payments for each, and generally calculate the payoff dates.

NOW, you can throw extra money at the littlest one at any time. So, don't be in a rush to tackle it if you are unprotected. I don't want you to fear debt, just don't plan to stay there forever. If you create your emergency fund and sit down to define your snowball plan, you will be in great shape to get your debts paid off while you continue to operate with ease.

USE the worksheet to plan out your debt snowball, and to get an estimate as to how long it will take to become business debt free. This timeline can also help you plan for future growth in your business! I always recommend that entrepreneurs limit the debt on their business. Debt and tax issues are the two critical financial issues that force business closures. We closed UNEQ for a different reason, but we absolutely struggled with debt and taxes. I don't want that for you.

HAVING the combination of a Cyclical Fund, Emergency Fund and a debt elimination plan will help to protect your business operations for longevity. Remember to revisit your C-fund and E-fund deposits whenever expenses or annual fees change. This way, you can adjust your balances to keep that entire blanket of financial protection on your business.

THE DUMP Your Debt Planner

STEP 1: List debts, payments, and number of months to pay

CREDITOR:_____ Balance:_____
Payment:_____ Months:_____

CREDITOR:_____ Balance:_____
Payment:_____ Months:_____

CREDITOR:_____ Balance:_____
Payment:_____ Months:_____

. . .

CREDITOR:_____ Balance:_____
Payment:_____ Months:_____

CREDITOR:_____ Balance:_____
Payment:_____ Months:_____

CREDITOR:_____ Balance:_____
Payment:_____ Months:_____

STEP 2: List from lowest to highest balances and attack the littlest debt with the most cash you can allocate. Pay the minimums on everything but the little one. When that debt is paid, add the payment from the littlest debt to the next minimum payment and snowball that payment amount again when it's paid in full.

DEBT 1: _____ payment:_____ PIF
date:_____

DEBT 2: _____ payment _____ + SB
payment_____ New pmt:_____

DEBT 3: _____ payment _____ + SB
payment_____ New pmt:_____

DEBT 4: _____ payment _____ + SB
payment_____ New pmt:_____

. . .

DEBT 5: _____ payment _____ + SB payment_____ New pmt:_____

DEBT 6: _____ payment _____ + SB payment_____ New pmt:_____

NOTES:

THE TRUTH ABOUT PROFIT

"You were born to win, but to be a winner, you must plan to win, prepare to win, and expect to win."
Zig Ziglar

*I*f you have followed me for any length of time, you know that my number one rule for business is, "Don't Lose Money." Now, this doesn't mean we never make money mistakes; rather this means that we are deliberate in our pricing and costing, so we are moving into profit with everything we sell. Not only do I want you making money, I want you making and keeping *a profit* in your business.

I ONLY LEARNED ABOUT "MONEY MINDSET" work a little over a year ago. It turns out that the way you view money and your money story has a huge impact on how you manage money and on your financial decision making. Without a good money mindset, your potentially negative financial patterns will return over and over and can derail your progress. Let's talk about the most common money mindset mistake I see entrepreneurs make when they are starting out.

Your Money Mindset Affects Your Profit

"If I make too much, I'll be seen as greedy."

"My business is for people who don't have a lot of money."

"I should just price myself lower so I can make more sales."

"I'm kind of new, so I need to stay at a lower price point so I can find clients."

I've heard every one of these phrases over and over, and I have also said them myself. The truth is, you are in business to make money and earn a profit. There is nothing morally wrong with making a profit. In fact, *profit* equals *impact*. The more profit you make, the bigger impact you will have in your community by hiring more people. In your circle when you can support other small business owners by making purchases from them. In society, because you will be able to support causes and organizations that are important to you. You cannot do these things if you are broke or running a charity with your financial approach.

. . .

DON'T MISUNDERSTAND ME. I want you to have ethics and good values. They are important for everyone, and especially for doing good business. I want you to come from a place of deep service and to be in business because you have a passion to bring your gifts to the world. I also want you to make the money you want and to make your business into your vision. Whatever your vision may be, and it takes money to do that.

I CAN GO on and on about my mindset and perspective shifts since I started doing this work. The best recommendation I can make is for you to get into the "I Heart Money" course by Emily Williams and really examine how your beliefs about money are holding you back. Money is morally neutral. We put value on it, both good and bad. If you want a thriving business and to have the money to make a real impact in your community, you need to do this foundational work.

"I DON'T NEED THAT MUCH" is the cry of the resistance. But you aren't in business only to fulfill your needs. You are also in business to create profit and to reach your financial goals. If you don't have yours defined yet, let's write down some profit goals and the why behind them.

TIPS FOR WORKING on Your Money Mindset by Financial Personality

MONEY MINDSET WORK has to be done daily and can be challenging if it isn't a habit or you don't have the greatest relationship with money. For a brief reminder of the personality types, review Chapter 1.

- If you resonate with Annie: Money mindset work requires that you pay attention to your money; and if you have everything on autopay, you aren't giving it enough attention. You can view money as a good friend, someone you have to build a relationship with. And you will also have to build trust that money will always be there.

- If you resonate with Sally: You need to learn that the ways we make money aren't necessarily linear. Your calculations will get you so far, but the universe gives us opportunities that we didn't see coming. Money mindset work here requires that we be open to receiving and looking for the opportunities, not just relying on the numbers on the page.

- If you resonate with Olivia: Money has to be something you see in the future, as well as in the here and now. Your money mindset work should include exercises for looking at how you will spend your money in the future. You can begin to build an expectancy that will help you be more comfortable with planning for your finances.

- If you resonate with Jessica: If you are struggling with the money month over month and trying everything, you need to look at your money story. What were you taught about money? What do you really think about people who have money? You may be blocking your relationship to money with unexamined money beliefs that create hardship.

WHAT IS Profit and Why Do I Want It?

I LOVE the show on CNBC where Marcus Lemonis is, "The Profit." He invests his own money and knowledge to help turn around struggling small businesses. Something I hear in the show over and over relates to money issues such as, "this business generated $4.2 million last year but had a loss of $30,000." Many people can't understand how a business making millions can be losing money, and that tells me that many, many entrepreneurs do not know the difference between generating revenue and cash, and making a *real profit* in their business. This critical gap in understanding is costing small businesses millions, creating financial problems that put small businesses in jeopardy of closing.

IT ISN'T About the Money You Make; It is About the Money You Keep

How can a multi-million-dollar business post losses? Because having sales doesn't mean you will have anything left after all of your liabilities. Just because it sold millions doesn't mean there is a positive balance in the bank after the business pays salaries and expenses, and services any debt the business may hold.

This is why I am so passionate about helping you make sure your pricing, expenses, and offers are right, so that you not only make money but keep more of it. More profit means more growth, more impact, and more service.

Business Revenue and Cash

Sales generated for your products and services are your *revenue* and the physical money you collect is *business cash*. The more sales you are making, the more you bring in every month. That is the first half of the equation. Basically, every physical dollar that comes into the business is business cash. Other sales on payment plans or installments count towards revenue but aren't yet sales in the business as "cash" until the payments are made.

THE KEY IS to have profit, that amount of money left over every month.

"GROSS PROFIT" AND "NET PROFIT"

Gross profit is the difference between your cost to create your offer, product or service, and the retail price you sold it for. For example, the materials and labor to make your widget costs $7.00, and you sell it for $15.00. Your gross profit is $8.00 per widget. This is the number many entrepreneurs rely on for pricing and for expenses. But it's the wrong one.

WHAT'S MISSING in this number is the amount of the "hidden" expenses, such as all of your operating expenses of rent and utilities, plus taxes. Let's say your operating expenses add an additional $2.00 to the cost of each widget: *your net profit, after all expenses, is really $6.00 each.* That $6.00 is the one we want to know, and it is the one to work with when we look at growing the business.

Start By Ensuring Every Product or Service is Profitable

Do the quick math and make sure that everything you sell is generating a profit, an amount left over after everything. Remember that your profits don't have to be equal for every offer; one offer can be 10% profitable and another 25%, but each one must be profitable on its own.

PRICING

So, how do we calculate selling price so that we don't lose money?

First, I want to acknowledge that there are many different ways to price goods and services: Value Pricing, Cost-Plus Pricing, and Market Pricing, to name a few. There are great free pricing calculators on the web; if you like excel spreadsheets there are some calculators with pricing formulas available as well.

I am honestly just a "Keep it Simple, Stupid" (KISS) kind of girl; after all, I was in the Navy. Unless you are manufacturing or have a multi-tiered pricing structure, you can calculate the selling cost of your product and service fairly simply, and come up with pricing that won't allow you to lose money. Here's my quick 3-step method for checking your pricing. If you are in manufacturing or have more complicated pricing models, you can still use this method to calculate your operations costs and ensure you are recovering those!

STEP 1: LIST ALL OF YOUR COSTS.

I mean ALL. Do you print labels for your handmade goods or buy tags for pricing? It counts. Gas to get to the flea market? It counts. Pay for an online platform or storage for all of your digital products? It counts. Beads and wire for your jewelry? List the costs for each style. In your pricing, I want you to recover ALL of your costs. Some of these costs may be captured in your Breakthrough Number, and if they are, we will address them in operating costs. However, sometimes things get over-looked. I have worked with too many entrepreneurs who were leaking profits 10 cents at a time because they forgot to add some actual cost for each product or service sold. So, list your *real* costs for each product or service.

STEP 2: CALCULATE YOUR BUSINESS OPERATIONS COST.

You want to know how much it costs you every day and every

hour to be in business. Add up your Breakthrough Number and other costs, and get a total monthly amount; or just use your "All-in" number. Take the monthly total and divide by the number of days you are open each month, then number of hours.

FOR EXAMPLE, if you are open every week in the month, divide by 4; this is your weekly operating cost. For a daily operating cost, if you are open 5 days a week each month (5 days in four weeks), divide your all-in number by 20. For an hourly operating cost, if you are open 8 hours a day, divide again by 8. This will give you your hourly operating costs. This operating cost must be recovered in every pricing decision.

STEP 3: ADD A PROFIT MARGIN.

Go ahead, add 10%. I'm not saying your costs plus 10% is your price for everything, but I want you *right now* to start thinking about profit margin. So, add a profit margin!

ONCE YOU KNOW YOUR COSTS, your profit margin, and your hourly cost of business operations, we can calculate what you should sell your goods and services for. Let's say your wholesale cost for all the materials to produce your jewelry is $35.00, and it costs you $23.00 an hour in operations cost, and it took you an hour to produce that piece for sale. You want a 10% profit margin, so we add another $3.50.

. . .

THE PRICE for that piece of jewelry should START at $61.50. Of that amount, only $3.50 is truly profit. So, if you are selling for $40.00 (costs plus a little bit) you are probably losing money. And we need to fix that. There are several ways to do it, through proper pricing, cutting expenses, etc., because you are probably losing money if you don't. And rule number one is, "Don't Lose Money."

MORE ON PRICING for Service Providers

MANY ENTREPRENEURS' low ball their prices for products and services in the beginning. I did. For my own story, I had a coach who told me what I already knew; I was undercharging. Imposter syndrome is a real thing, and many of us tend to undervalue ourselves and the impact we make in the beginning of our entrepreneurial journey. This seems to be very common with service providers.

COACHES, consultants, and freelancers typically start lower than they should, and are sometimes slow to raise prices. Profit margins in service businesses are typically higher than many product-based businesses because there is no physical product for sale. Because there isn't a "wholesale" cost, so to speak, many of us struggle to price our services. And if we don't have a responding increase to the cost of doing business, we tend to struggle to "justify" a price increase to ourselves.

There are a lot of articles and methods for pricing yourself in the marketplace, in addition to ways to raise your prices. What I want to offer is a way to raise your prices when you are resisting such increases by identifying the increase with a name. Just as we did earlier, we'll simply call it the "profit line." This can help with some of the hesitancy to increase prices: your "base price" remains the same, but you add on an increase and have a real purpose for the money.

You decide what you want to add as a percentage. For example, you charge $200.00 for a service. You add $20.00 as a 10% pure profit line, so the new price is $220.00 for your service. Your prices are raised, a bit, and moving forward every time you sell that service, you siphon off $20.00 to put into an account for profit. Give that account a name, a purpose. You don't have to stop at 10%. You can add 50% profit and make your service $300.00. Your decision.

If you are resisting raising your service prices, give this method a try. Figure out how much profit you will have in an account in a month if you add this line. Plan your next business move. What is this specific profit amount going to be for? Remember that any money without a name will run off and spend itself. Go ahead and raise your prices. Just do it. Add a profit line this week.

Here are 5 Additional Tips for Maximizing Profits

Beyond addressing any pricing issues, there are other places your business may be losing profit. Your time, costs, delivery, sales discounts, and lack of follow up with potential customers may be costing your business real money. Here are some tips for addressing these sneaky profit leaks.

1. MANAGE YOUR TIME

Your time has value. The longer you spend on things that

aren't revenue generating, the more profit you can lose every day. If you have a process to make widgets, for example, but you are interrupted every 15 minutes to answer emails or to take calls, the time it takes you to produce the widget is longer, but you aren't getting more money for the widget!

The time interruption takes you off task, and actually costs you real profit! Make a list of everything you have to do and decide what is actually going towards making money. Use time blocking to manage your schedule and prioritize those things that make your company money. Delegate the things that aren't generating revenue and are not in your zone of genius.

2. MANAGE YOUR COSTS

Every time you pay for something you don't need or will not use, you are taking money from your profit. Perhaps it's a subscription that you are no longer using or maybe you haven't looked at your suppliers in a few weeks or months and their prices have creeped up, or you have gotten into a groove and haven't looked at your expenses in a while. It is important to be as "lean" as possible in business to keep as much profit as possible. Every unused subscription at $12.95 a month adds up! Review your processes at least once a year and check your providers for new or different capabilities and packages. Are there places to streamline to one provider, or to change providers that allow you to be more efficient in your process?

3. MANAGE YOUR DELIVERY PROCESS FOR YOUR PRODUCTS AND SERVICES

When you coach clients, do you typically go over time? Do you run to the post office every day to mail orders? Is your process clunky in returning emails to customers who have questions or problems? Do you have a client flow process from onboarding to completing your service or product delivery?

Your delivery process for your products and services can directly impact your profits.

If the processes are not clear and there are inefficiencies anywhere along the line, this will eat into the profits you are creating. Keeping your process as simple as possible while giving legendary service is crucial.

4. WATCH THE "FLASH SALES" AND CUTTING PRICES TOO OFTEN; IT CAN LOOK LIKE DESPERATION

When sales slow, your immediate instinct might be to cut prices and try to make money on volume. Every time you cut your prices, you cut profit. I know, offering sales prices can be great for business, *but do it with a plan.* If you get desperate every month and hold a flash sale the last week, your customers will get smart, and wait until then to order.

Plan your sales and tie them back to some business purpose. Are you holding a sale to add customers to your list? Or maybe for a product or service launch? An early bird?

Cutting prices early and often is a recipe to eat your business profit.

5. THERE IS MORE MONEY IN YOUR FOLLOW UP.

I recently read that over 80% of sales are in the follow up, after

5 contacts. So, have a follow up process. Whether it's an email newsletter or email nurture sequence, a plan for phone call contact, the follow up is critical to the sales, and therefore the profit your business makes. Additionally, it is easier to keep a client than to acquire a new one. You can resell products and services to your existing clients with less effort than gaining new ones.

AS I'VE MOVED to more online business, I've realized that I'm actually pretty bad at this one and have been working hard to create a good system for myself. I know it is critically important. If you are here, it's because you are trying to maximize the profits in your business, right? You want more growth and impact.

ACTION STEPS TO **Take Now to Protect Your Profitability**

1. Make sure you are pricing everything for profit and check your current prices *now*.
2. Plan your sales discounts and tie them to your greater business plan. Making a quarterly income and profit plan is a great way to map your offers and how they affect your money.
3. Check your costs and expenses at least twice a year. Rerun your Breakthrough Number and check the prices of your suppliers. A few hours online may save your business big bucks and make you more profitable.
4. Have a plan for the profit. Know your purpose for your profit goals and celebrate when you reach them!

CREATE MORE REVENUE

❧

"A pivot is a change in strategy without a change in vision."
Eric Ries

Creating more revenue in your business begins with setting your financial goals.

"When you aim at nothing, you will hit it every time." – Zig Ziglar

Why We Need to Set Goals

FIRST OF ALL, goals tell us our desires. Goals help us to separate the wishes and dreams from the things we are willing to work towards. Without goals, we can't channel our ambitions. Goals are often tangible, so we can stay motivated through the process, as we reach different milestones on the path to the ultimate achievement we want to attain.

If you aren't in the habit of setting goals, I encourage you to do so. Here, we are talking about increasing revenue. How much more do you want to earn? How quickly do you want to earn it? Answering these questions will help you start to put financial goals in place so you can maximize the process of finding more sales opportunities, which we cover later in the chapter. You can make decisions to pursue one course of action over another by knowing what your money goals are.

THERE ARE many different ways to set goals. You may approach them differently if you are setting a goal for your business versus your personal life. The important thing is to have them and have a clear reason *why* you are setting them. A popular approach to setting goals uses the "SMART" strategy. That approach requires all goals be "specific, measurable, achievable, relevant and timebound." I don't align 100% to this approach, but find certain elements are universal in setting any goal if you want to achieve it.

I HAVE no problems with the "specific and measurable" parts of this approach because you have to know the end state you will work towards. As for "timebound," I start by identifying the end state of my goal and backwards plan, putting steps on the calendar to create a timebound *strategy*. For example, if I am setting a financial goal, I give myself a specific amount of money with a timeframe to hit it. In practice, this includes an overall deadline and several "check in" deadlines along the way for evaluation and progress checks. Progress is motivating.

I BREAK with the SMART method on the topic of, "achievable." For achievable goals, I think it is helpful to look past what we know we can do. Sometimes we shy away from setting goals that we aren't sure we can hit. Many people sell themselves short on what they can really reach. I think if we set "achievable" goals too narrowly, people won't undertake a "stretch" goal, the one that is just outside the obvious reach that forces us to work a little harder or be a little more creative to hit.

ONCE THE GOAL IS SET, however, it must become non-negotiable. I recently started reading, *"The Audacity to Be Queen"* by Gina DeVee, and she explains it as, "being unavailable for anything else." When you use your desires to set your goals; rather than working from a position of "I wish, I want", your starting position is "this is happening, this is what I am doing." We commit to taking each action step with unwavering determination and belief. And then start moving.

SPECIFICALLY SETTING Financial Goals

I OFTEN SEE two distinct approaches to financial goals by business owners. Some have vague goals because they just want to sell, "as much as possible." So, they don't set anything specific. Other entrepreneurs set super stretch goals that they can never reach, with the belief that, *"if you aim for the moon and miss, you will land among the stars."* I understand both approaches, and often, they don't work. I want to offer you an approach that falls somewhere in the middle.

If You Don't Typically Set Goals Right Now

Start with the end in mind. How much money do you want to make, and in what timeframe? Does answering those questions have you thinking right away, "What if I set it wrong? Too low or too high? Am I going to be disappointed? What if I miss it?", I hear you. The fact is, goals don't have to be arbitrary or decided by throwing a dart at a bunch of numbers. Here are a few questions to help you narrow down a good goal.

1. WHAT AM I OFFERING, HOW MUCH DOES IT COST?

How many can I sell? This question will help you look at your capacity to make more money. This may be limited by your time, by your production model, or by your own working guidelines.

If you don't know the maximum that you can comfortably make with each offer in a month, you can't begin to set a very accurate goal, because you can't figure out what to sell and how many. Take the time to look at your capacity because it will not only cap your income but also your ability to scale.

2. WHAT IS MY BEST SALES MONTH EVER?

What made it so good? Was it a new ad? Did you host a challenge? What was it?
These questions can help you to examine what you did in your best sales month, and whether you can duplicate it or do more now. What are you available to do to hit your goal this month?

3. WHAT IS THE PURPOSE FOR THE MONEY?

Having a purpose can definitely help you gain clarity on your goals. If you want to make $3,000.00 so you can launch a new thing, then that's a pretty clear purpose for the money. Get laser focused on what you want the money for and what it is going to do for you and your business when it is earned.

If You Tend to Set Super High Goals That You Always Miss

First, examine the three questions. And check on your capacity, availability, and purpose for the money and the goal. Then ask yourself if it would be better to keep the lofty goal as a "best" goal but add in a "good" and a "better" goal that is more attainable.

FOR EXAMPLE, if you set your goal at $10k for the month, but your best month has been $2k and you don't have the availability to do more than $6k, you can set a "good" goal at $3k (attainable) and a "better" goal of $6k, the "best" (or stretch) goal of $10k.

THERE IS a real psychological boost to you as an entrepreneur as you reach your financial goals. For each of the three goals, make sure you have a clear purpose for the money. It takes just a few minutes to set your financial goals. It can be for the week, month, quarter, that is up to you. But make sure you have something to aim at and then define the availability and steps you need to take to hit your mark.

Setting Financial Goals Based on Your Personality

Planning your financial goals can be challenging if it isn't a habit or you don't have the greatest relationship with money. To refresh your memory of the financial personality types, please revisit Chapter 1.

- If you resonate with Annie: Start to set financial goals by writing down small, reachable goals. If you aren't used to making goals at all, you need to take baby steps to make it a habit. Revisit the goals throughout the month; set a day of the week to review where you are, and really get intentional with setting a goal monthly!

- If you resonate with Sally: You probably tend to set goals looking only at what you will accomplish. But making goals looking only at your own actions misses the opportunity for bigger growth and bigger goals. Don't be afraid to invest in support to meet your big goals. Hire the VA or the social media support. Don't be afraid to have a stretch goal and get the support to reach it.

- If you resonate with Olivia: Planning for the future is sometimes tough for you because you are always reaching for the next thing, which is great, but you are just winging it. Start to implement a tangible goal each month, such as the amount of money you will make or the number of things you will sell, and have a plan for the money when you reach that goal.

- If you resonate with Jessica: Making a financial goal is great, backing it up with the action steps to get there is even better. You may already set goals each month, but you may be struggling to reach them each time because you are going after the goal inconsistently or without action steps. Backwards plan how you are going to accomplish your goal, with concrete actions, and stick to it this month.

WHEN WE MISS Financial Goals

I said "when" not "if" because, at some point, you will miss your goals. Business is dynamic, and things happen. It never feels good to make goals, work hard towards them, and miss them. A lot of people like to use the "miss the moon, fall amongst the stars" analogy to describe missing your goals, but the fact is, most of the time, it hurts.

THERE ARE people who believe that, if you don't hit a goal, you didn't want it badly enough. Maybe. I think if you don't hit a goal, any number of things could have happened. Have you ever gotten halfway to a goal and then lost your passion for the result? How about external forces that interfered? Ever have a goal that you reach at another time? How about something that needed to be tweaked, something you will correct for the next round?

WHEN YOU DON'T HIT your goals, it isn't the end of the world. Because you made the goal non-negotiable and you are unavailable for anything else. Any perceived "miss" is a timing issue. Or an approach issue. You need to find the lesson. You need to evaluate what went well, what didn't, and you need to be willing to make adjustments and to continue moving forward. Replace any disappointment with a celebration of your progress. A genuine celebration.

FINALLY, sometimes missing your goal can be a great thing. It opens your creativity. It forces you to look at your path, planning, and approach. Missing and reaching goals teaches a valuable lesson in every attempt and every victory. And with the right perspective, you will see that, in your efforts, you either meet your goal or learn something that changes you.

Creating More Revenue Requires Generating More Sales

THE CONCEPT of the business pivot is not new. I learned about it several years ago when I was in the Syracuse University V-WISE program for women veteran entrepreneurs. Traditionally, a pivot is a term to describe a strategy to turn a business when the current business model isn't working. A plan "B", if you will. But I also see a pivot as a strategy that can aid expansion of a business. I don't think a pivot is only a plan B, but can be a *business strategy* for small turns, little twists that steer the business to look in an additional direction.

A PIVOT often comes about because something isn't working or isn't working as well as you want it too. Many times, businesses start with one business model and shift, or pivot to another. A "pivot" isn't a bad thing, it's the smart thing. Maybe you aren't seeing the progress you want, or the revenue isn't growing. Maybe you just sense something is "off" with your vision. Most businesses have adjustments and changes, a "course correction" if you will, before finding their envisioned "success." Business success is about differentiating yourself from others in the marketplace, so a "pivot" becomes another business strategy.

THE PROBLEM IS, many entrepreneurs just dig in and keep trying the same thing "harder," often bleeding cash in the process. It might be helpful to think of the pivot as the open window to save the fly repeatedly banging its head into the window. If something needs to be "tweaked", the right pivot, no matter how slight, might grow your business and increase revenue. The key is to make the RIGHT pivot!

ENTREPRENEURS ARE, by nature, change agents, known for figuring out ways to do things better, ways to take calculated risks. We are also known for continually searching for the "next thing." *I believe that using a simple pivot analysis can help you find the next move for your business.* Again, I don't ascribe to a pivot as something to do *only* when things are going wrong. I believe that a little turn deserves a pivot analysis, so risks can be weighed in a structured, but simple, way. Use this three-step process to discover your next business move.

1. *Commit to use openminded and unfiltered brainstorming.* For best results, use the recommendations by Jennifer Jackson of <u>Lucid Chart</u> and just get every idea down on paper; and edit later.

1. *Use the Entre Money Coach ADFP Formula.* Ask open ended questions about your Audience, Delivery, Focus, and Processes for places to improve, serve, and expand.

1. *Use market research to explore ideas.* Don't just throw out unusual ideas as bunk. Do a little market research to see if there is a fit. There are all kinds of free resources online to help you. Don't forget to look at adjacent industries and at your own industry for ideas and changes going on that can support your ideas.

Some of the best business moves are those that seem to be a natural twist or progression. A pivot doesn't have to be dramatic to positively impact your bottom line.

THE ADFP FORMULA

YOU CAN EXAMINE four major pivot areas for big changes by using the Entre Money Coach ADFP Formula. In this method, you will look for opportunities for greater growth and revenue through changes to your Audience, Delivery, Focus, and Process.

Audience: the customer you identify and sell your product or service to
Delivery: the manner in which your product or service gets to your customer
Focus: your product or service
Process: how you serve your customer, start to finish, through each sale

To FIND the area for a potential pivot, simply answer the following questions. Allow yourself to brainstorm and write anything and everything that comes to mind. There will be time later to sort through and decide which actions you want to take first, and which ones don't seem to fit with your business. Start now, and give yourself permission to expand your current markets, products/ services, and how you serve!

AUDIENCE: **Who are you talking to?**

- ARE your ideal clients returning as repeat customers?

- ARE recent customers ones that you didn't originally identify or market to?

- Are you getting requests for products and services from a different demographic, such as age group?

- Can you identify the newer members of your audience? Are they a different type of client?

DELIVERY: How are you serving?

- Do you get requests to provide your product or service in a different manner? For example, adding online shopping to your brick and mortar boutique, or creating a package for your salon to offer in addition to individual services.

- HOW CAN you offer products and services differently?

- Do you see your industry moving into a different delivery of products or services to the marketplace?

CHECK out this Toolsrush article (https://www.toolsrush.com/free-market-research-tools/
for a list of 25 tools for conducting market research to look at your industry.

FOCUS: what are you selling, and how?

. . .

- ARE your clients asking for something different than what you offer?

- Is one product or service doing better than expected or better than everything else? Perhaps you could add more of the popular focus or expand!

- CAN you bundle or repackage products and services to create new reasons to buy?

- Is your industry offering something that you do not, that your customers expect and ask for?

PROCESS: Are your clients supported and served well?

- DO you have multi-step processes that can be simplified to improve customer service? For example, add an online appointment system in addition to accepting phone appointments.

- DO YOU HAVE AN IDENTIFIED "FLOW" to move each customer through the sales process from lead to following up after the sale?

- DO you need to add a process to reduce sales "friction," meaning making your product or service easy to purchase? For example, add online payments for customers or perhaps a payment plan over a few months for a package.

. . .

Do You Really Need to Pivot?

THE ENTRE MONEY Coach ADFP Formula was developed as a personal tool because I have been through numerous pivots over the years. My most recent pivot is an audience change; I split my personal financial coaching from my business financial coaching. In fact, you could say that this resource is a function of the second audience question, "Are you getting customers you didn't originally identify or

market to." My answer was yes. I started receiving inquiries and getting clients who were entrepreneurs.

ENTRE MONEY COACH is the result of personal coaching several clients with small businesses. I learned that they wanted more coaching and support in the business, to help their personal financial situation. I responded and my primary audience changed.

WHEN YOU HONESTLY ANSWER THE questions, do you see one area where a shift or pivot would be a good fit? If you identified more than one area, dig a little deeper into your answers. You are looking for the smallest change with the best results. The purpose of a pivot is to change what isn't working so well, without major business structural alterations and with minimal cost to your business, so you can serve your customers with the things they want to buy while providing legendary service!

CHOOSING YOUR FIRST Pivot

Once you have all your answers down on paper, you can look at them all, sort all of your ideas into the ones you will take action on, ones you will hold off for a few, and some that don't really fit. You will likely want to start taking action on the pivots that are the fastest and cheapest to implement.

FOR EXAMPLE, I had a client that produced amazing handmade soaps, creams, scrubs, and other personal care items. She had an audience of loyal customers, but her products lasted so long her resales were infrequent. After some ADFP analysis, we decided she should make smaller sized products and bundle them for the purpose of selling gift sets. There wasn't any real change to her time or money to implement this idea. She already had the containers. So, she chose the three most popular flavors and started selling gift sets to her existing clients in addition to new clients who were looking for a gift for occasions such as Mother's Day. She created a new reason for people to buy from her with just a slight audience and focus shift. Adding gift packaging created a new delivery pivot, adding a few dollars for the bag and ribbon.

EVALUATING the Cost-Benefit and Return on Investment

GRAB a piece of paper and make two columns. List the easy and cheap ideas on one side, those that need more effort or money on the other. Before you decide to implement any idea that will cost the business more time or money, you will want to do a quick analysis of the cost-benefit of using the idea.

. . .

EVALUATE each idea you wrote down, one by one, and determine what resources you will need to put each idea into practice in your business. Also estimate time that it will take to be fully available for your business. For example, if you wrote down "online course" in your delivery analysis, evaluate how long it will take to create the content, where you will host and what that may cost, the time for marketing and creating a sales page, etc. This will help you make decisions by weighing what you have to put out in resources and what you get back, and how quickly from your efforts and financial investments.

There is another factor to keep in front of you as you move through this process. We have to be honest with ourselves first about what is important to us. When you evaluate your ideas, don't look purely at the dollars and percentages. Did any of your ideas include new efficiencies? How about projects that will take a little time to set up but allow you to serve more people? Make sure you look at the end result, as well as the time and dollars.

IF THERE ARE any ideas that came up during the brainstorm that you don't think you will implement at all or don't seem like a good fit, you can decide whether to throw them out or if you want to keep the notes for now. I have personally revisited my own analysis and used certain ideas later on in the future. This book is a perfect example. This was part of a delivery analysis over a year ago!

YOU CAN ALWAYS CHANGE IF IT ISN'T WORKING

My coach has a great expression that, "You aren't getting a tattoo on your face." And, unless you really are, you can change anything once it starts. As your business matures and grows you may find some processes or team members don't fit your current ROI evaluation. You shouldn't feel bad about that. I have seen some business owners who hold onto a business decision a little too long. Typically, because they don't want to "upset the apple cart" and hurt someone's feelings. You can change suppliers. And you can change social media managers. You can do all the things you need to as you are staying true to your vision. You should re-evaluate ROI regularly as you are making the next set of decisions to move forward.

ACTION STEPS TO Create More Revenue:

1. Set your income goals, you can start with monthly and then quarterly

2. Take the time to brainstorm through the ADFP Formula to spark ideas and to discover sales opportunities

3. Sort through your ideas and pick one to run though a cost-benefit analysis

4. Implement your idea and create more sales in your business

GET A BOOKKEEPER AND AN ACCOUNTANT

❦

"If you think it's expensive to **hire** a **professional**, wait until you **hire** an amateur."
Red Adair.

This short chapter provides you with some basic info to get organized for tax times and demonstrate how I take care of my self-employment taxes in the U.S. I am not an accountant or tax pro. I've had small business accountants since we started UNEQ in 2011, and bookkeepers on and off since then. I do not handle my own taxes. I feel that having the right professionals makes a ton of sense in this space, whether accountants, bookkeepers, payroll companies, or financial advisors. You don't want to make too many mistakes here. I speak as someone who had an IRS lien on my house, paying all of the penalties and interest charged because we knew we were at fault.

· · ·

MANY TIMES, I speak with entrepreneurs who have "turned all that stuff over" to an accountant, meaning, they don't look at or control their business money. I get it. The money stuff isn't as sexy as a new logo or website. The truth is, your bookkeeper, accountant, or payroll company is NOT responsible for your bottom line. They are responsible to keep you compliant and out of trouble. Here is my take: You control the income, let your accountant do the accounting. Let the bookkeeper run the eaches and make the entries. You don't have to complete your own Profit and Loss statement.

THESE SMALL BUSINESS professionals SHOULD take care of the reporting and advise you on the best way to manage your responsibilities as they pertain to taxes, withholding, unemployment insurance, etc. But they are NOT invested in making sure your profit margins are "right." That's YOUR job. The thing is, YOU have to control your income. Don't delegate that part of your business.

YOU KNOW WHAT COMES IN, and decide what goes out, to whom, and when. You pay your own self-employment taxes (unless you are an employee of your company). That's it. Let your payroll company cut the checks and deposit your employer taxes. Let your accountant help you plan for and file your taxes, and keep you compliant and legal.

THE RULES for reporting self-employment income are straightforward. If you are a sole proprietor or a single member LLC, you must report your self-employment income and pay taxes using a Schedule C when you file your 1040. If you have a corporation or an LLC with more than one member, you must file a different form.

THE FOLLOWING section is intended for the US based small business owner who files a Schedule C, takes a paycheck but is not incorporated where the entity withholds the Medicare/Social Security taxes. Always consult a tax professional to ensure that you are meeting your legal responsibilities as a business owner as it pertains to taxes. If you are unsure whether you need to deposit for yourself, get clarity right away! Penalties and interest are added by the IRS if you fail to meet your obligations.

THE BASICS: Your Self-Employment Taxes in the U.S.

IF YOU ARE new to business, or don't already have your self-employment tax system set up, this section is for you. Many entrepreneurs treat taxes as an afterthought, often because cash flow is tight, and they don't hold back personal taxes when they take a paycheck. In the US, self-employment deposits are for Social Security and Medicare taxes, like those that are withheld from your paycheck when you are employed. When the IRS speaks to self-employment taxes, it is referring to this type of tax. There may be additional taxes that business owners and self-employed people have to file.

The rates for self-employment taxes may seem high when you first start paying your own. For the 2019 tax year, the self-employment tax rate was 15.3% of net earnings, meaning after your expenses. The truth is that, when you have a job, the employer must pay about half of the tax expenses for its employees. So, generally, the same percentage is paid by every-one. But if you are employed, you pay half (7.65%) and your employer must pay the other half (7.65%). That's why it seems like so much more when you pay for yourself.

You must withhold your taxes and deposit them at least quarterly. This is where many small business owners run into problems. The rules don't allow for self-employed people to just pay annually; you must deposit quarterly, or you can face late-payment penalties.

Setting Up a Simple Tax System To Stay Organized

Here is a simple process for setting up your ongoing tax system for success.

Pay Self-Employment Taxes Regularly Online. You can easily set up to deposit your taxes online through the IRS Electronic Federal Tax Payment System www.EFTPS.gov by enrolling in the program and receiving a PIN from the IRS. Once you are enrolled, you can deposit your taxes online whenever you take a paycheck. If you get into the habit of writing yourself a regular paycheck, and immediately withhold your self-employment taxes, you will simplify your accounting and reporting for the end of the year, and keep yourself protected from tax issues.

Many business owners make quarterly deposits. You don't have to pay your taxes quarterly. Just make sure what you paid in each check totals what you owe by the end of the quarter. If you always deposit 20%- 25% this shouldn't be a problem. This is what I do, I don't hold back and deposit quarterly anymore. I deposit online every payday.

Stay organized with your expenses. Your business taxes are calculated on your NET income, meaning after expenses. Keep your receipts organized, perhaps in an envelope by month, and put the total on the outside of the envelope for each month. You can easily keep a running total of your expenses on a sheet by totaling the expense envelopes. This doesn't have to be complicated!

The Best Way to **Find Your Money Pro**

Finding your money pro is important for the health of your business. You need a bookkeeper and an accountant, and perhaps a financial coach, but who should you look for? Get a few recommendations from people you trust and make sure you interview each candidate prior to making a decision. A good match is going to balance your strengths and weaknesses. Here are some things for you to consider as you find your money pro based on your financial personality.

- If you resonate with Annie: you need someone who will take the time to explain to you exactly what has to be done, the importance of it, and to help you prioritize so you meet your deadlines and goals. Because the tendency is to ignore your finances, it's best to have someone who will send you reminders, like a monthly email.

- If you resonate with Sally: You need a collaborator who will share the data regularly. You want to know the P&L and you should have it on time. This person has to balance you out, though, by giving you a timeline when things will be available and sticking to it. And no stressing in between! Let this trusted person be your financial wing person.

- If you resonate with Olivia: You need a good planner in your corner, someone who will help you stick to it. They send you reminders to file taxes and pay them. These pros will ensure that you are looking to your financial future. Your tendency to only take care of what is in front of you requires someone who can see the bigger financial picture, quarter by quarter.

- If you resonate with Jessica: You need someone to help you set up the nuts and bolts of your system, and to help you stay on track. Most of the time, it's merely the case that you don't pick something because you aren't sure what to pick. Let your pro take a look at what will work best with your personality and your interests.

Helping Your Accountant: Staying Organized for Tax Time

You can make tax time painless for you and your accountant this next year by staying organized throughout the year. When I submit my information to the accountant, I hand over a single folder for each business, with income, routine expenses, deposits made, and any other pertinent receipts. He receives the totals and prepares the proper forms. I keep the individual regular receipts and have them in case of an audit.

1. TRACK ALL INCOME IN A SINGLE PLACE.

Some people like to use software, some like Excel spreadsheets, some get reports from PayPal, for example, and some use good old-fashioned pen and paper. If you use a payment processor like PayPal or Stripe, you can run a printout at the end of each month that provides you income totals and the amount of interchange fees you were charged. You need to account for every dime coming in, and it's best to look at it month by month.

I meet way too many entrepreneurs who don't actually track the money coming in. They just set up to pay the expenses on auto pay and use a credit card to cover any negative cash flow. The issue with this approach is that you can't track trends or opportunities to make more money. It further makes quarterly tax deposits a pain. I recommend to my clients that they take 10-15 minutes every week to track that gross income number.

2. KEEP YOUR ROUTINE EXPENSES ORGANIZED.

THINK of these as the expenses that make up your Breakthrough Number. You need to keep everyone and everything you pay for every month in one place. This serves two purposes: First, you don't forget to pay something, and you have all of the info at your fingertips if you need to contact a creditor. Second, you can use the expense organizer from Chapter 2 in this book to make your list of monthly expenses and track your monthly payments to each one on a spreadsheet, app, in software, in a notebook or using any other written method. At the end of the year, you will have your total for your routine expenses such as rent, phone, internet and software.

3. ORGANIZE YOUR OTHER RECEIPTS BY MONTH.

THE EASIEST WAY TO keep receipts organized is to tackle them once a week, as they come in. If you track everything by week, you will have 4 tracking sheets a month with all of the associated receipts. You can use my 90-day Undated Money Management Planner, a spreadsheet, an app or a notebook... whatever system works best with your personality and that you will stick with. On an envelope, write the month on the front. Every expense receipt for the month goes into the envelope. Then the receipt amount and purpose of the expense goes on a monthly tracking sheet. If you buy ink for the printer, for example, write "ink" on your tracker, with the amount, and put the receipt in the envelope for the month. The same for "annual license renewal," for example. At the end of the month you can write the month's expense amount total on the outside of the envelope.

THAT'S IT! At the end of the year you will have 12 envelopes with every expense and 12 months of tracking. Beyond keeping tax stuff organized (and never losing a deduction), this tracking can also be used to spot trends in costs and other things that you can use for business planning.

4. ENROLL IN EFTPS AND DEPOSIT YOUR SELF-EMPLOYMENT TAXES ONLINE.

FOR TAX TIME, you will just print out a summary of payments to the IRS and include it in the documents you give your accountant. Easy peasy.

By taking these few actions, consistently tracking your income weekly and your receipts once a month, you will be organized and ready to provide everything to your tax pro.

ACTION STEPS TO **Take Care of Your Taxes**

1. Enroll to pay your taxes online. This way, you can print out a record of your deposits at the end of the year and give it to your tax pro.
2. Have a weekly and then monthly system for tracking income and expenses.

3. Keep one folder or envelope for receipts each month and note the total amount of the receipts on the outside.

4. Hire an accountant who understands small business. You want a pro who can help you with deductions and allowable expenses.

TAKING A LOAN TO INVEST IN YOUR BUSINESS

❦

"Invest in your mindset. Invest in your business. Invest in
yourself."
Jill Celeste

I get this question frequently: "When is it the best time
to take a business loan?"

MY ANSWER IS: "IT DEPENDS."

IF YOU HAVE BEEN in the online space for any length of time, you
have seen all of the posts and ads urging you to "invest in your
business." I agree that it is wise to get expert help to shorten a
learning curve, get help to support you in tasks that are outside
your zone of genius, and to grow the business so you no longer
exchange time for money. When most entrepreneurs start a

business from scratch, they are bootstrapping for quite a while as they refine their niche, products, and services for market.

THE TRUTH IS, 69% of small businesses are started at home, and most of the time personal income, savings, or credit cards are used to start the business and support it in the early stages. Mike and I started UNEQ Consulting with personal money, and I worked for a bit at my job as Mike got the contracts we needed before I would go full time in the business. I also started two other businesses this way, at home with personal income. I know many others who have, as well.

WHENEVER SOMEONE ASKS me about making an investment, it is because the dollar figure needed is higher than they have cash for. And many times, it can be higher than available credit. So, an additional source of funding must be found to get the coaching, marketing, consulting, new equipment, or other needed support. With the exception of businesses like franchises or those that require expensive equipment to start producing items for sale, such as a restaurant or certain manufacturing industries, most businesses can start slowly and become profitable without significant startup expenses.

I TOOK a business loan for the first time to hire a business coach to help me, and I leveraged my car to do it. As you read in Chapter 5, I was dead set against getting a loan at all, but the learning curve was very steep getting into the online space and, admittedly, I needed tons of mindset work and support to get out here after Mike's accident and the UNEQ consulting experience. One thing to note is that I had already made some sales and knew that coaching and strategy support were the next step for me to shorten the learning curve and make more revenue.

IN SHORT, this chapter is all about taking loans to grow the business after it is already making some revenue. I always ask entrepreneurs to consider whether they need to make an investment before they have proven what they want to do has market value. There are some amazing coaches and consultants who can help you identify your niche, help you pivot if needed, and create a very marketable product and service. And there are others who are not so good at this. I recommend that you at least have a few sales and offers under your belt when you invest a large sum of money in your business. This doesn't mean you shouldn't buy the course or the templates or join a membership of like-minded professionals. Those purchases aren't typically in the price range people are concerned with.

TAKING TOO Much Debt Too Soon

IF DEBT IS TAKEN TOO early or too much is borrowed, it can kill your business. Debt is a huge reason many businesses fail. Large debt payments can become a financial burden that is too much to overcome when you are just starting and beginning to grow. In those cases, the entrepreneur can't generate enough revenue for all of their obligations, because of the addition of loan payments to the monthly expenses. Once you have some consistent revenue into the business, it is much more likely that the business itself will make the monthly debt payments; which can also ease any fears of paying the business debt with personal income.

. . .

BUSINESS DEBT, unlike consumer debt, cannot be discharged in bankruptcy under Chapters 7 and 13 under the U.S. Bankruptcy Code. You will have to pay the debts back that are taken for business purposes. This is a surprise to many people because they often have to give a personal guarantee for the debt, but the test is not who guaranteed the loan, rather the purpose for the money. Any business debt must be filed under a different bankruptcy code, chapter 11, and there are different rules around what can and can't be discharged or reorganized.

TAKING Debt For Your Business

HERE ARE a few considerations before taking loan for any investment. I want to stress again that it is best to take out loans to grow the business, not pay for business expenses. It is always better to pay your monthly expenses from the business or personal money, a side hustle, or even another business rather than borrow to pay the rent or inventory. When I took out my loan against my car (using collateral not only made it easier to get but gave me a lower interest rate), I was paying to grow the business. I wasn't borrowing money to pay expenses each month.

1. DO YOU HAVE A PLAN FOR EVERY DIME YOU BORROW?

WE SPOKE EARLIER about money needing a purpose. When you are going to borrow money, you also need a plan. I'm a huge fan of planning and have a project management background. I know that planning isn't easy for some people, or it may seem overwhelming. But this step is critical.

YOU WANT to make sure that you are requesting enough. If you don't figure out exactly how much you need, you may not have enough to finish the project or course and see the results. On the other side, I see entrepreneurs get approved for credit cards and loan amounts that exceed what they really need to make the growth jump. You should only take what you need, and you should have a plan for *all* of it. Money without a purpose will run off and spend itself, and this is borrowed money. You owe it back.

I TEACH the basics of project planning and how to plan your revenue and profit in several courses and workshops. I'm going to give you a quick method for mapping out a plan to ensure that you take exactly what you need to meet your goal. I want to make sure you don't take too much or too little. If you want to have a "cushion" of about 10% of your project or growth need in the bank, just let it sit there and do not spend it. Once you complete the project, you can pre-pay the loan. Just make sure there are no pre-payment penalties.

HOW TO CREATE a Plan

A PROJECT HAS a definite beginning and a definite end, and you can create a plan that takes you through the project because of this fact. I have a four-step process that will give you a quick mind map and allow you to create a budget that will guide your loan request.

- Step one is simple. Describe what you want the end state to look like. Are you creating a new offer or product, or joining a mastermind program that will help you get to the next level? Start with the end in mind.

- Step two is to list all of the tasks to complete the project. For example:
- Create the item or package or service
- Determine price
- Create marketing products/value statements
- Add to payment portal or create an invoice
- Choose a launch date

- Step three is to put all of the tasks in the required order of completion. Order them by what gets done first, second, third, etc. Add timelines to each task and note any resources required for each task. This is where you want to estimate how much you will need for each task that requires financial support.

- Step four is to backwards plan and calendar the tasks and timelines. This does two things. It creates a roadmap for each piece of the project and can help you look at the costs over time. Once you have this together, add up all of the estimates and you have what you need to ask for a loan.

I CREATE a project plan for almost everything, whether I am developing a course or taking on a team member to help me with a tech project. It helps me get the tasks and their associated costs organized. It also provides me with a step-by-step process for getting everything done on time to meet my goals.

2. DO YOU HAVE THE CAPACITY TO MAKE THE LOAN PAYMENTS NOW?

CALL ME OVERLY CAUTIOUS, and maybe I need to work more on my money mindset and manifesting, but have a way to make the payments before you take the loan. One common mistake I see when loans are taken is the assumption that once you make the investment, you will immediately make enough to make the payments. That happens a lot of the time, but in reality, we don't know how long things are going to take to make a return. When you decide to take a loan, remember that you are leveraging the future of your business until you pay it back. When I took out my loan, I already knew that I could make the loan payments, without issue, from my other business venture if necessary.

THERE ARE several ways to find the money for payments before you sign the loan documents. It is time to be creative and look at all of your options. Not only where to find the money but to make the payments themselves in a range that feels comfortable and is doable for you and your business.

. . .

HOW LOW CAN you make your payments? I opted for a 36-month loan because I knew I could make the payments and I didn't want to feel like I was dragging the loan out forever. This probably had to do with my past experiences, and this was the loan term that was right for me. But maybe your budget works better with 48 months? If you use a credit card, can you get a zero-interest option for a certain length of time? That way you can start with minimums, but add to the payments as you make more money, a la debt snowball?

WHERE CAN you find the money now to make the payments? Can your business afford them now? Do you have a personal income source, like a job that can pay for the debt? Do you need to pick up a side hustle temporarily as you grow your business? When we were digging out of debt in 2014 and 2015, I was working part-time for an online market research firm. I made a few hundred dollars a month. That monthly amount would make payments for most small business loans.

IT CAN BE a good thing to invest in your growth, cut the learning curve, purchase what you need to be able to serve more customers and clients, and expand your impact. Use loans for growth, have a plan, and have the capacity to make the payments before you start. I want to see you investing money and taking business loans in the right way!

BUILDING THE BUSINESS IN YOUR VISION

"Chase the vision, not the money; the money will end up
following you."
Tony Hsieh

Stepping Into Your CEO Role: Adding To Your Team

IF YOU ARE RUNNING A BUSINESS, you are a business CEO, and it
can be hard to see it at first and hard to grow into. Actually, I
recently coached a client who was still doing *everything* in her
business, just like we all do when we start, because she wanted
to make "more" before she delegated some tasks. These days,
you can get recommendations for temporary support for almost
any business related task. You can look for project contractors
and freelancers who are on Fiverr and Upwork. The fact is,
there is a mindset shift when you see yourself running a business and not just as a self-employed person.

. . .

As the CEO, you will do the research and set a financial goal to get that new team member or contractor in place. As the CEO, you have a vision for your company that goes beyond paying yourself a comfortable living. To bring that vision to life, you must step into the role of the company leader. So, how did we address my client's need to step into the CEO role?

First, I asked her to define "make more" before you begin to hire out certain tasks that are not in your zone of genius. "More" is an ambiguous term and an amount you will continue to raise because you can. You can never reach it because you didn't put a line in the sand. "When I make $2500.00 every month, I will add a _____ fill in the blank…" is much better than, "I will add a _____ fill in the blank… once I make some more."

Next, we made a list. What do you want to get off your plate first? Her answers were bookkeeping (a top fave for most entrepreneurs!) and social media. Awesome! How can we get this done as fast as possible? Here are a few things to think about:

1. YOU CAN START SMALL.

You don't have to hand off everything all at once. For example, hire someone just to schedule your social media content. The hour it takes to schedule a month of posts is an hour you can be making sales, creating items, generating leads or just being in your zone of genius. You can get something off your plate

NOW. Think about it and start small. What can you hire out this month?

2. YOU ARE YOUR BEST BRAND AMBASSADOR.

A KEY to letting go a bit and getting started with a team is to understand that *you are the best person to make the sales,* to promote your company, to generate the leads, to build the brand. You are sold out to your vision or, if you aren't, let's get that way. If you are scheduling posts, writing newsletters, book-keeping, creating graphics, etc., you aren't doing the major things that grow the company. Like making the sales.

Let someone else do the things that aren't directly related to your making money for your vision.

3. IF YOU ARE NERVOUS ABOUT THE MONEY, WHAT IS A COMFORTABLE BUDGET?

IT IS ALWAYS NERVE WRACKING to take on a new expense in your business. Many times, we allow fear to stop us from boldly stepping into the CEO role because we may not "make enough next month." If someone quotes you a number that gives you hives right now, what is your *comfortable* budget? Have you ever given it a thought? And back to number one, if your budget is truly small, start with just one thing.

YOU ARE THE VISIONARY, and you have the vision for the company. Where are you going? You cannot get there if you are bogged down doing everything for your business by yourself, particularly as things start to take off.

MAKE the decision today to step into your CEO role and make the plan for the next stage of your business. Remember, you can switch from self-employed to business CEO. It just takes analysis and good prioritization.

SCALING

WE HEAR THE WORD, "SCALE" thrown around a lot in business, particularly online when they say you need to scale your business. According to The Startup Finance, it means: "Make more revenue faster than it takes on costs." Using that definition, you want to start scaling as soon as possible. That is how you can become more profitable because you will have more income at a ratio to lower costs. That is actually always a good place to be in business. Here are a few tips you can start using now if you want to start scaling your business.

1. YOU CAN CREATE VERY LOW OVERHEAD PRODUCTS THESE DAYS

ONE WAY TO add revenue with minimal costs is to create a digital course or product that can be sold online. Another popular low overhead service is online memberships. By adding revenue, and not adding costs to produce each item, this can help to scale your business quickly. You are serving more people without taking on more costs.

. . .

2. YOU CAN CREATE MULTIPLE REASONS TO BUY FROM YOU WITH MULTIPLE OFFERS

AGAIN, without increasing costs, you can create a new offer that can be resold to your existing audience. Or perhaps an existing offer can be repackaged for gifts. Or maybe you can add a fun bonus to an offer and give your audience a new reason to buy from you. You are serving your same people again without taking on more costs.

3. YOU CAN KEEP THE COSTS LOW BY MINIMIZING DEBT

SMALL BUSINESSES and start-ups can begin to scale more quickly if they keep business debt very low, or if possible, non-existent. Using my Breakthrough Number approach, everything above the business four walls is profit, and from that amount, we must pay debt. Without debt, you have more revenue and more money going into those profit parking lots.

4. SCALING CAN CAUSE SHORT TERM BOTTLENECKS TO PUSH THROUGH

THIS IS one side effect we don't talk about but, as you are generating more and more revenue, if your systems aren't in place, it may cause a bottleneck where you can't generate more or serve more without more money for systems. It happens; a way to minimize this risk is to have some support in place as a temporary or project-based cost until you get to the next income level. You cannot scale all by yourself. You need support.

5. ALWAYS WATCH YOUR PRICING

INCREASING revenue without being aware of any potential profit leaks can defeat some of your scaling efforts. Generating income at a faster rate than you take on expenses is a beautiful thing! Keep your eyes on the profit margins as your business expands.

Remember that every line of business should be profitable, but they don't all have to be equally profitable.

EMBRACING Growth

YOUR BRAIN LIKES to keep you safe. It likes to talk you out of doing things that are new and perceived as "dangerous." Like opening a new business, meeting a new income milestone, or launching new products and services. If your brain doesn't have a point of reference for the "new" thing you are doing, it defaults to believing you are in "danger" and it takes immediate steps to talk you out of it, putting doubts, fears, and sometimes self-sabotaging behaviors into your head. To make you stop. To keep you "safe." It's all laid out in *The Big Leap* by Gay Hendricks.

It's happened to you before. It has happened to all of us. You get a great new idea and immediately you think, "This will never work." Or you have repeatable patterns of self-sabotage every time you are ready to launch something new into the world. It's frustrating and confusing. Why does the brain work so hard to derail anything new? Even if the new thing is good for us, like making more money?

It's actually quite simple. Our brains haven't adapted to the fact that we aren't physically in harm's way when there's something happening the brain doesn't recognize. The ego wants to keep us in the status quo where it can predict everything, and nothing is going to harm us. This is the part of the brain that watches for cheetahs chasing us. And it hasn't adapted to life today in the 21st Century. But you can get past an upper limit problem. We need to get past the brain's safety switch so we can level up past our previous "set point".

FIRST: ACKNOWLEDGE THAT THIS IS NEW, AND YOU KNOW THE BRAIN IS FEELING FEAR.

Recognizing an upper limit problem is the first step. Paying attention to how you feel and what's going on around you as you begin to do or attain something new and different is the first step. Fear may show up in different ways, but the consistent thread is that your brain is trying to talk you out of moving forward and is making excuses for you not to continue. We've all done it, had those inner conversations that talk us out of ideas.

SECOND: REASSURE YOUR BRAIN THAT YOU ARE SAFE.

Give it a little attention and thank it for trying to protect you. I thank my brain all the time, and remind it that I am safe, and that we are doing this thing. By paying attention and not ignoring my brain, the negative voices in my head do quiet down a little. It is okay to feel scared when we try something new. Anything new in our business may feel scary, and in many cases, we are unsure of the outcome, no matter the projections and plans. Acknowledge it. Remind yourself you are safe.

ANOTHER TRICK IS to trace and minimize the fear by asking, "What if (this negative thing) does happen?", and answer the question. For example, "what if we don't sell any?", then honestly examine the consequence. By answering the questions, you give yourself a point of reference. By giving yourself a point of reference, the brain can calm down.

THIRD: DO YOUR THING. JUST DO IT.

YOUR BRAIN WILL CREATE a new set point as it experiences your new level. As you try and succeed or learn different things, the brain adapts and knows "how" to do it, and it isn't seen as automatically dangerous. I have my own upper limit problems. We all do. I tend to self-sabotage when "new" things are happening, and the business is readying to break through a level. Your brain will sometimes cause your body to hurt or get sick to keep you from getting to the next level because it doesn't have a frame of reference and wants to pull an emergency break to stop you! In fact, I spent time recently on bed rest from an odd back injury. I didn't fall and don't remember hurting myself, but I had a bulging disk in my lower back. Is this my body and brain telling me to slow down? I think it was. So, I now go a little slower. But I am not quitting, which is what my brain really wants me to do.

· · ·

FOURTH: RECOGNIZE THE GROWTH PLACE AND CELE-BRATE IT.

WHEN YOU GROW and reach the next level, celebrate it. You've done it now, your brain has a frame of reference, so you are not going to struggle at that level again. FINALLY, RINSE AND REPEAT. Every time you come up against something new or scary, you will likely have to calm your brain and give it reassurance. It is a part of growing and making permanent changes in your life. And once you are aware of them and take the steps to grow around them, your growth potential is limitless.

THE MULTI-PASSIONATE ENTREPRENEUR

I AM A MULTI-PASSIONATE ENTREPRENEUR. Across the businesses, I am a teacher, coach, and cheerleader, but each busines is very different and has very different audiences. I teach and coach entrepreneurs with their money and strategy, I tutor and coach non-traditional law students through school and the bar, and I teach ballet, tap , and jazz one day a week. And I am passionate about each one of my ventures. I know there are some of you out there who are just like me. I wanted to take a minute and support you by providing a few tips and tricks for balancing the finances across entrepreneurial pursuits. We will start with the "rules."

- Rule number 1: Every venture is different: you must separate your finances. Period. I have accounts for each business. I have check books for each business. I go so far as to have Stripe for one and PayPal for another to process payments. The money is earned in different businesses. By using PayPal, I can also "park" the money until I need to transfer it. No co-mingling. I keep everything absolutely separate. So should you.

- Rule number 2: Expenses are different and should be tracked separately for each venture. This is as easy as putting all the receipts in a different folder, one for each business. Make sure that you pay the right expenses from the right account. Another benefit of PayPal is that I can send money directly from the business account to pay expenses. You can set up the same for your businesses. Keep them separate.

- Rule number 3: Taxes are separate in each business. You must pay the self-employment taxes on each venture. If you are a sole proprietor in the US, you will have one EIN if you are operating with your own social security number. You can make a single tax deposit online to cover the taxes for all three, but you must keep withholding separate in your tracking. You must file a Schedule C with your taxes every year for each business that you own as a sole proprietor. If you are an LLC, Limited, S-Corp or any other structure, you must absolutely deposit your own taxes but let your accountant do the proper filings at the end of the year.

It doesn't have to be complicated for the multi-passionate

entrepreneur. I sit down and handle each business separately and in turn I have a written spending plan for each, and the B-number that goes with each. I spend less than 1 hour a month on the financial planning and management of the companies.

How to do it:

1. Have Your B-Number. Know your B-Number for each business separately and have a written spending plan for each. I'll say it again: know your breakthrough numbers and have a plan for the money in each business. If you need to calculate your breakthrough number, get the free workbook at entremoneycoach.com. This step will save a ton of stress and crazy. You know what you need to make, what you need to pay, and where your money is going.

1. Use color coding. I have different colored folders for each business. I mark receipts as I get them and place them in the correct folder by color. To avoid payment errors, I have checks in different colors with a little icon in the corner. Color coding keeps everything easy and organized. You can find different colored folders and markers at any office supply store.

1. Delegate what you aren't good at, or don't like to do. Stay organized with a virtual assistant, bookkeeper, accountant, etc. The actual bookkeeping

for my businesses is very straightforward, and I don't do it. My accountant takes less than 3 hours a month for all the businesses. I only manage the income and planning.

1. <u>Always have a plan for your money.</u> Don't let your money run off and spend itself. Know what each business's income is for. Your money every month must have a purpose. You may decide to take a salary from one business, with the intent to use that salary to grow a different one. Have a plan, withhold your taxes, and use your money strategically.

I celebrate multi-passionate entrepreneurs like me and understand that being organized can sometimes be a challenge. But take the few steps just detailed to make managing the finances across multiple businesses easier. Happy Entrepreneuring!

REMEMBER That You Will Always Be Evolving

WE ARE in business to make impact, AND to make a profit. The more money you make, the bigger the impact you will have. To continue to grow and reach more and more people, you must be willing to continuously evolve and strategize. Business is fluid and dynamic. You must be open to changing. Remember, you can always evolve while keeping a core focus or product. This isn't to say that you have to change everything, rather, you must be open to changing the things that affect your growth and impact.

MIKE'S ACCIDENT changed everything I thought we were going to do. It changed my trajectory to consumer law and financial coaching. And it has helped me become a much better business-woman than I would have been if UNEQ was still running.

To start, I am ten times better and more successful when it comes to business planning, strategy, and managing as a CEO now.

UNEQ operated (rather successfully) from a lack of real planning as to the direction of the company. We had client projects, yes, and a calendar for execution, but I cannot remember a single time Mike and I sat down and asked, "Where are we going this quarter, and how do we get there?" This lack of planning was quite a liability when the company closed because we didn't have an emergency fund or continuity plan, so we had to turn back all of our contracts. All $375k worth of contracts.

Now, I make sure that the annual, quarterly, and monthly planning is done. What is offered, when, how much we are bringing in, the content we are putting out, and when I need to add another hire. I make the time to create a business strategy, not just sales and marketing, to drive us toward the future I see for Entre Money Coach.

I ALSO GIVE myself a regular "CEO space" to step into powerful successful business- woman energy. That is just time to brainstorm and be with myself and my vision for the company. This is the time I let myself develop a higher-level plan and I have the 3-year and 5-year goals for where we are going.

I Always Try to Operate From a Place of Service, Knowing There Are No Coincidences

I believe that people are put in our path for a reason. I didn't believe it back then. We lived in a company bubble and believed that people existed because we had a great team and great project execution. One thing UNEQ suffered from was a tinge of arrogance. We were good at what we did, not too many companies did it, and we were thriving on referrals and without marketing. It made us a little bit too confident. We took risks we shouldn't have, didn't always pay attention to the finances and, because we always had another contract coming, allowed our personal lives to sort of suffer. We operated from contract to contract, doing a great job, but not from the perspective of being in service to our clients.

Today I operate from a completely different place. I have become better because I see myself first as being in service to my clients. Sometimes that means a lot of handholding, sometimes it means a little bit of tough love, but it is always in service to their company and financial goals. I see myself as on a mission to help my clients become as profitable and successful as they desire.

Now I Make Decisions Without Fear or Regret

During the UNEQ years, I spent way too much time worrying about making decisions and worrying about making mistakes. I would game plan 100 different things and constantly second guess myself when I finally chose to do something. For this reason, Mike made a lot of daily and weekly decisions.

My fear of failure was to a level of causing anxiety. After the accident, I was put in charge of making the decisions surrounding closing the business, Mike's medical care, and anything else related to our daily lives. I actually didn't always get the chance to think about failing, I just had to make a decision and we moved on it.

MY COACH, James Williams, declared, "You either win or you learn." I resisted this for a long while. I was still wavering a lot on making decisions for Entre Money Coach. Do I hire the social media support? Should I pay a copywriter? For the first months, I struggled with this. I lost the art of making decisions the way I had in the months following the accident.

BUT I STARTED TO EMBRACE, "You win, or you learn." There are no mistakes, and I don't have time to regret. I do the planning, the due diligence, and I have clear goals for this journey. So, I just decide. And I keep moving forward. This is my fondest hope for you.

REFERENCES

Gillaspie, Dixie, Entrepreneur.com, November 2014.
  https://entrepreneur.com/article/239701

Internal Revenue Service, Employer Identification Number, apply online. https://www.irs.gov/businesses/small-businesses-self-employed/apply-for-an-employer-identification-number-ein-online.

Your Federal Business Number in Canada.
  https://www.canada.ca/en/revenue-agency/services/tax/businesses/small-businesses-self-employed-income/setting-your-business/sole-proprietorship.html

Your Unique Taxpayer Number in the United Kingdom.
  https://www.gov.uk/browse/business/setting-up.

The Seven Baby Steps, Dave Ramsey online. https://www.daveramsey.com/get-started

REFERENCES

The Entre Money Coach Payday Newsletter link: https://entremoneycoach.com/payday

Online Pricing Calculators in Excel:
   https://exceltable.com/en/master-class/calculation-production-costs

On the Importance of Goal Setting, Why You Need to Set Goals, Keep Inspiring.me, https://keepinspiring.me/why-you-need-to-set-goals

5 Characteristics of the Entrepreneurial Spirit, Matt Ehrlichman,
   https://inc.com/matt-ehrlichman/5-characteristics-of-entrepreneurial-spirit-html

How to Brainstorm: 4 Ways to Get the Creative Juices Flowing, Jennifer Jackson, Lucidchart online. https://lucidchart.com/blog/how-to-brainstorm

Top 25 Free Tools for Conducting Market Research, Toolsrush online.
   https://toolsrush.com/free-market-research-tools

5 Reasons It's Important to Have an Accountant for Your Business, Bizjournals online.
   https://bizjournals.com/bizjournals/how-to/growth-strategies/2015/04/5-reasons-why-your-business-needs-an-accoountant.html

IRS Electronic Federal Tax Payment System. www.EFTPS.gov

Adding to your team. These are websites where you can look for independent contractors and freelancers for projects.

Fiverr. https://fiverr.com
Upwork. https://upwork.com

What is Scaling in Business and How is it Different Than Business Growth? Lighter Capital Blog, May 2019. https://lightercapital.com/blog/what-is-scaling-in-business

Hendricks, Gay, *The Big Leap,* Harper Collins e-Books, April 2009.
Order on Amazon: Amazon.com: The Big Leap: Conquer Your Hidden Fear and Take Life to the Next Level eBook: Hendricks, Gay: Kindle Store

Williams, James, Coach, I Heart My Life, https://iheartmylife.com

ACKNOWLEDGMENTS

I need to thank the amazing people who helped make my manuscript into a real, live book.

I couldn't have done it without the editing support of my dad, David Silverman, who retired after 47 years in the business only to come out of retirement to support me. I am grateful.

I want to thank Marie Miller for her design support and for talking me back off the ledge here and there. Your friendship is invaluable to me. Thank you.

I also want to thank Wendy H. Jones, the international best-selling author who I met on another writing project. She formatted this entire work, has the best resources for marketing a book, and gave amazing advice when I needed it.

Last but not least, I want to thank my husband Mike for his part in our story and for always being my biggest fan. I love you.

ABOUT THE AUTHOR

"Dawn Kennedy is an attorney, financial coach, author, and serial entrepreneur who is passionate about helping small businesses thrive in the face of unexpected market changes by ensuring there is a plan to protect financial milestones and a plan for the company's successful growth. She gained an extensive background in program management and strategic planning working for the US Army and as a consultant for companies in both the government and private sectors.

Her focus on financial coaching began when she faced some tough financial lessons with UNEQ Consulting, LLC, a six-figure consulting business she ran with her husband Mike. On November 1st 2013, Mike had a near fatal fall 18 feet off of a ladder, and by the grace of God he survived, but their company did not. Mike went into rehabilitation and they were forced to confront the stack of bills they could no longer pay. It took 39 months, but they paid the business and personal debt off at a total of over $76,000.00.

Today, she applies the lessons learned from UNEQ and her training as a financial coach, project manager, strategic planner, and attorney to work with other entrepreneurs to implement positive and powerful changes to help their businesses thrive and grow. Dawn solves problems with creative options that get results.

On a personal level, Dawn is a is a wife, mother of 5, grandma to 3, a hero to her three dogs, and a US Navy Veteran.

f ⊙

www.ingramcontent.com/pod-product-compliance
Lightning Source LLC
Chambersburg PA
CBHW061827040426

42447CB00012B/2847